SACRED
LEGACIES

Past Lives, Present Dreams
The Hidden Power of Dreams
Sacred Space
The Secret Language of Signs
Quest

SACRED LEGACIES

*Healing Your Past and
Creating a Positive Future*

DENISE LINN

Ballantine Wellspring
The Ballantine Publishing Group • New York

A Ballantine Wellspring Book
Published by The Ballantine Publishing Group

Copyright © 1998 by Denise Linn

All rights reserved under International
and Pan-American Copyright Conventions. Published
in the United States by The Ballantine Publishing Group, a division
of Random House, Inc., New York, and distributed in
Canada by Random House of Canada Limited, Toronto.
Originally published as *Descendants* in Great Britain by Rider,
an imprint of Ebury Press,
Random House UK Ltd., in 1998.

Ballantine Wellspring and colophon are trademarks of
Random House, Inc.

http://www.randomhouse.com/BB/

LIBRARY OF CONGRESS CATALOGING-IN-PUBLICATION DATA
Linn, Denise.
    Sacred legacies : healing your past and creating a positive future /
Denise Linn. —1st ed.
        p.   cm.
    Includes bibliographical references and index.
    ISBN 0-345-42515-4 (alk. paper)
    1. Life.   2. Quality of life.   3. Spiritual life.   I. Title.
BD431.L4297   1999
291.4'4—dc21   98-37037

Text design by Holly Johnson

Manufactured in the United States of America

First American Edition: February 1999

10 9 8 7 6 5 4 3 2 1

I dedicate this book to my daughter, Meadow Marie Linn.
She is my descendant, and it is for her that I wrote this book.

Contents

Acknowledgments

This book grew out of an intense passion I have for creating a more humane world for my daughter, her children, and all future children. Although the magnitude of the spiritual and environmental crises facing humanity may require bold and visionary methods, I know in my heart that it is possible to find solutions to our planet's problems.

I wrote *Sacred Legacies* to provide practical information, which anyone can use, to help create a positive future. I believe that each individual, no matter what his or her circumstances may be, can make a difference. Great movements start out in small ways, and even the mightiest rivers are made up of an infinitude of single drops of rain. All our actions together, all our hopes and dreams surging into a mighty river of consciousness, can create a better world, one we can feel proud to pass on to future generations.

The concepts that form the basis of this book came, in part, as a result of the rich experiences I have had within my extended family. It gives me joy to acknowledge my family, for through them I have come to a deeper understanding of myself. It hasn't always been easy, but the value I have gained has outweighed the challenges. I acknowledge: my grandparents, Jenny and Hamp Scudder and Roy and Gladys Fortner; my father, Dick Fortner, and his wife, Edna Fortner; my mother, Jean Fortner; my aunt, Galela Pisarra; my uncle, Wade Scudder; my sister and brothers, Heather Fortner, Gordon Fortner, and Brand Fortner, and Brand's wife, Monica Fortner; my stepsisters and their husbands, Chellie and Mike Kammermeyer and Sandy and Jeff Grafton; my husband's parents, Alvin and Harriet Linn; my husband's sisters and their husbands, Susan Linn, Terri and KC Anderson, and Sandi and Alan Levi. I especially want to acknowledge my husband, David, and my daughter, Meadow.

In addition, the assistance, support, and inspiration of Claire Brown made this book possible, and for this I am enormously grateful. I'm also very thankful for the information that Nundjan Djiridjakin (Ken Colbung), Credo Mutwa, Joseph Winterhawk Martin, and Brand Fortner so kindly shared with me for this book. Also, much love and thanks to my friend Lele Galer and to my editors, Judith Kendra and Joanne Wyckoff.

SACRED
LEGACIES

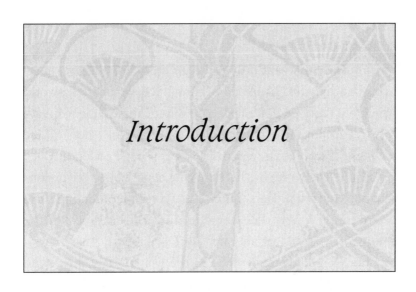

Introduction

In every deliberation, we must consider the impact of our decisions on the next seven generations.

—FROM THE GREAT LAW OF THE AMERICAN INDIAN IROQUOIS CONFEDERACY

The journey to write this book began fourteen years ago when an informal survey was taken at my daughter's school about the children's view of the future. The results were disheartening. Many of the kids stated that they were afraid they would not grow up to be adults. The reasons they gave for this fear ranged from worry about nuclear disasters to environmental catastrophes and gang violence. When I voiced my dismay about these responses, I was assured that the results were not typical of all children because the survey had only been taken at an urban public school.

I was not comforted by their reasoning. It seemed to me that the sentiments of these children reflected a disturbing undercurrent of fear and negativity about the future in our culture at large. I frequently encountered these same attitudes in adults, so it did not seem to me that this was an isolated phenomenon relevant only to urban children. Nagging questions continued to haunt me. "How have we created a world where our children don't feel safe? What can be done to create a better future for our descendants? What can *I* do?" These feelings did not lessen over the years as I searched for answers.

Fear of the future has become part of our collective unconscious. As we approach the end of one millennium and the beginning of a new one, numerous individuals proclaim the coming of the end of an earth cycle. Some say that Mayan prophecies predict catastrophe in the year 2012. Others state that Nostradamus predicted a "holocaust" around the turn of the millennium. Many proponents of New Age philosophy express their belief that this will be a time of catastrophic earth changes and upheaval. Numerous born-again Christians declare that the millennium will be the time of the Armageddon. Some environmentalists predict global environmental catastrophes. I once attended a New Age conference where the panelists were posed the question, "*When* will the cataclysm come?" not "*Will* there be a cataclysm?" This question was based on the disturbing premise that a coming cataclysm is a certainty rather than one of many possibilities.

Fears about nuclear holocaust, the poisoning of our planet, overpopulation, and the potential for other global disasters have eclipsed our sense of connection to the larger context of life: our own future and the future of our children and grandchildren. For some, perhaps the allure of imagining worldwide destruction can obscure the potential for a positive future, which may seem somewhat mundane by comparison. However, the importance of resisting this preoccupation with doom cannot be overemphasized because whatever is expected tends to be realized in our lives. In the face of huge potential problems, it is easy to feel overwhelmed and insignificant. *This discouragement, if not fought and overcome through faith and action, has the frightening potential to make the predictions self-fulfilling.*

Believing in future disasters can contribute to creating them, if not on a planetary scale then most certainly in one's own life. An individual who expects the worst often has difficult experiences, while someone who expects the best in life often encounters wonderful opportunities. Human beings have a tendency to project their own inner process onto external circumstances. Many of the current prophecies allude to great floods: for example, it has been predicted that California will fall into the sea; huge tidal waves will wash over New York, London, Sydney, and Auckland; and the Pacific Ocean will cover the western United States up to Colorado, which will become a seaport state.

The waters of death are not a new concept. Ever since Noah and the flood, the universal symbolism of aquatic purification has been a prevalent and recurring theme. In Asiatic and Oceanic mythologies floods play an eminent role in absolution and purification. Even our present-day ritual of baptism uses water to wash away sins. Of course, there may be a possibility that the millennium will bring a flood that will cover one-third of the United States, but more likely, these prophecies reflect a universal symbolism that designates a personal need for absolution and purification. The individuals who categorically believe in a watery cataclysm may in fact be projecting their own personal needs onto the world at large. Many soothsayers of doom may be predicting their own upheaval rather than a global upheaval.

The spiritual leader of the Branch Davidians in Texas prophesied a fiery end to the world. Indeed, his prediction was accurate; however, it was *his* own world that ended in catastrophe through fire with the burning of his group's compound. If someone is spellbound by predictions of destruction, it may be a reflection of future changes within that individual rather than a global omen.

Stop and consider for a moment that even if a cataclysm were coming, would devoting your energy to fearing and preparing for it enrich your life today? I knew people in the late 1970s who were so concerned about the possibility of coming disasters that they isolated themselves in a mountain retreat and stockpiled food and guns. They reasoned that if people came and tried to steal their food after a disaster, they would be able to fight them off. Twenty years later these individuals are still waiting. Two decades of their lives have been consumed with paranoia and fear. Will fear of a cataclysm help deepen your relationships, build community with others, make you more tolerant and loving? What purpose does it serve?

The problems that we are confronting at this pivotal point in human history are real and they can seem overwhelming. In order to face and solve these problems, we need a vision that empowers us and helps us to feel connected with each other. Acting alone, we are impotent. Acting together, we can change the course of history. It has been done before. Changes in history often began as tiny personal acts that swelled into huge movements.

The choices we make in our own lives can help to create a powerful new reality for all humanity. By taking responsibility for changing the way we think about the future, by working in small ways to make a positive future more possible, we are co-creating that reality. When you choose *not* to become mired in hopelessness or to be mesmerized by potential disasters, that choice enhances the quality of your life and the lives of everyone around you. If we can collectively find a way to look forward to a bright and positive future for ourselves and our descendants, it can come about; and the way to that bright future starts with you. One stone doesn't make a dam, but thousands of stones can change the course of the mightiest river.

FOUR ACTS OF PERSONAL POWER

There are four acts of personal power that can positively affect the outcome of the future. First, we need to re-establish our connection to the past by exploring our roots and realizing that we are the product of a long and noble lineage of human beings who came before us. After we have taken this step, we need to sort through our heritage by embracing that which strengthens us, and by breaking negative ancestral patterns. Once we have done this, we can learn to shift our limiting beliefs about the future at a fundamental level. Finally, we are ready to take concrete actions to empower the future. Those going through this four-step process can make fundamental changes in their own lives as well as help to change the tide of history.

Connect with Your Past

The first step is to reconnect with our past. It is through initiating the process of remembering our connection to the sacred whole, to those who came before us as well as those who will follow us, that we can find the courage and human resources necessary to face the problems of the future. In order to establish this connection it is essential to find your roots. Where did you come from? Who are your "people"? Why are you here? Who are you? These questions can be better answered in the context of understanding your ancestral roots, for we all stand on the shoulders of our ancestors and those who preceded us.

Each of us is the distillation point of a great funnel in time that consists of the history, culture, and evolution of our species. What we have become is the result of thousands of years of individuals struggling, working, bearing children, and living their lives in the best way they knew how. The solutions they found to their problems are what made the reality of our lives possible. Sometimes they didn't make good choices, sometimes they failed at what they set out to do, but without them, we simply wouldn't be here.

Facing enormous difficulties and overwhelming odds is hardly a new phenomenon for human beings. Our ancient ancestors were confronted daily with problems much larger than many of us will see in a lifetime, such as starvation, death from common diseases and predators, and the possibility of being permanently disabled by relatively simple injuries. In facing these difficulties, our ancestors had at their disposal some tools that we have lost or forgotten. They knew that they were part of an unbroken line, stretching from the time before memory through them and on to the ones who would follow after them. They had a deep belief in the continuity of history. They had a strong sense of belonging to a community. Problems were faced as a group and didn't have to be endured alone. They believed that if they worked hard together, their actions were going to have an effective outcome. Solutions were sought which could work for everyone and could be passed down to the next generation.

Our society lacks this sense of connection to a spiritual lineage that could serve as an anchor for us, giving us courage in the face of great difficulties. Expectations of impending disasters are, in part, a result of our eco-social isolation. As this millennium comes to a close, many people seem to have lost the realization that we are all part of a hallowed legacy, a sacred continuum. We are both the descendants of our own ancestors and, in turn, the ancestors of those who will follow us.

Our sense of connection to the past has been swallowed up in the wake of the immense changes that have occurred over the past hundred years. We have gone from traveling by horse and cart to putting a man on the moon. Communication by letters and telegraph has been replaced by instant satellite transmission and the Internet. Mass transit has made the world into one global village, but it has also broken down local cultures. Few people will call only one place home in their lives. The average American family moves about once every five years. Although this mobility has increased personal options, it has also decreased our sense of connection to the places we live in and to the communities and traditions that exist there.

Our cultural values about what constitutes success and failure and how we relate to our families have been altered by the changes on our planet. The Industrial Revolution has sent parents to work many miles away from the home and often provides them with work that they cannot teach their children. The sanctity of the home has been replaced with a mobile society where education, entertainment, and even meals are frequently found outside the home. Opportunities for the elders to teach and train the young have nearly disappeared, and there is an ever-widening separation of the generations.

In our Western culture we routinely view the older generation as useless and a burden. Our elders are neither respected nor well cared for, and this disregard is reinforced by the growing sense of isolation from our human lineage. Feelings of isolation affect the very young as well as the very old. Families with young children no longer have the support of the extended family to help out in times of illness or when they simply need to get away for a while. Children often do not know their aunts, uncles, or grandparents, and they grow up having no idea what it feels like to be part of a large clan.

The changes that have occurred, and continue to occur, have taken place at such a rapid pace that there has been no time for either individuals or cultures to assimilate them. Change is not necessarily bad. Nature and societies go through change and upheaval as part of naturally occurring cycles, as part of the nature of growth. On a personal level, change and inner upheaval can sometimes free you from old, negative habits and stagnation. Change is an integral part of new growth, taking place in people, societies, and nature. However, the rapid change that is presently occurring has resulted in a rupture of our sense of connection to each other and to the past.

Our ancestors were better able to assimilate change into their lives because new events and challenges were incorporated into present patterns through the use of tradition and ritual. Rather than being overwhelmed by dozens of sources of ever-changing and often frightening news, ancient people passed on their "news" in the form of stories told around evening tribal fires. Potential problems, current events, and challenges were discussed and evaluated in view of ancestral history. This provided an anchor, a way of situating the present in terms of the past, which in turn provided a context for future decisions. A sense of tradition and the collective memories of past successes, as well as failures that were eventually overcome promoted feelings of security in facing difficulties in the present. Awareness of the line of a connection between all the generations—past, present, and future—ensured a sense of grave responsibility about the impact of present actions much further down the line. Re-establishing our connection to our ancestors helps instill a sense of a continuum that gives us a greater understanding of who we are and where we have come from.

Heal Ancestral Patterns

After exploring your roots, the next step is the discovery of negative family and ancestral patterns. Because we are not encumbered by having to spend most of our time just trying to survive, we are at a point in our evolution where we finally have the time to devote to breaking free from these negative patterns, so they are not passed down to those who follow us. The negative legacy from our predecessors can have a staggering effect on our emotions, especially if it is not addressed. To instigate change in our global family, we may need to infuse change in the family patterns that dwell within each of us. This means not only taking time to develop the positive influences you have inherited, but also releasing negative familial patterns so they aren't passed down. Healing the past helps restructure the present, which then becomes the hope for the future. By becoming aware of and breaking the cycle of negative family patterns, we help create a new collective unconscious, which is essential for the continuity of life on our planet.

Create a New Vision for the Future

The third step is the creation of a new vision for the future of the world. This is needed because our collective world has reached a crisis of perception. We have become myopic and lost the ability to see a distant future that is positive and bright. The rise of a new collective unconscious can truly begin with one person. The constructive acts and thoughts of even one person who does not adhere to the conventional ideology that decrees that our future is bleak can begin to effect a change of global consciousness. To change the world, it is valuable to release any negative beliefs you may have about our planet's future. We are all a microcosm for the macrocosm. If you can change some of your limiting core beliefs, you create an energy that emanates from you, touching the hearts and souls of those around you like ripples in a still pool. And, in turn, others around those people are affected as well. As you begin to feel a mystic link with the future, this helps others find their link with the generations beyond them.

Many of my ancestors were Native Americans from the Cherokee tribe, and for many of them a traditional time-frame was seven generations. This somewhat magical-sounding time period, which might in actuality span anywhere from one hundred to two hundred years, prompted the collective imagination of these ancient people to envision the people who would come after them. Thinking of time as units of measure progressing methodically forward into a far and unimaginable future is entirely different from imagining what your great-great-great-grandchildren's children might be like. The former leaves one feeling disengaged and even disempowered, whereas the latter immediately conjures up images, hopes, plans, and speculations that naturally tend to engender creative action in the present.

Take Action

The fourth step to fortify the future consists of taking action. Imagining what one's spiritual and biological descendants may be like can inspire one to embark on specific acts that can contribute to them. Every act, from planting a tree to recycling to creating a legacy to be passed on can make a difference. Of course, there are challenges facing the human race at this point in time; there always have been and there always will be. But instead of allowing those difficulties to diminish our dreams and our potential for heroism, they can inspire us. We can return to the ancient tradition of respect for the best of what has been handed down to us, combined with utmost concern for what will come after us.

This book represents my personal quest to find answers to the haunting shadow of fear I once saw in the faces of my daughter's classmates, mirroring the fear and hopelessness we all feel when confronted with the possible annihilation of our species. I believe that we must face and transform that fear into hope to create a positive, vibrant future for all of us. We must understand our roots, seeking out and honoring the best that our ancestors have handed down to us, so that we can compassionately empower our descendants to pass the torch far beyond us. It is my hope that you will join with me as we work together to make this vision a reality.

1

The Power of Generations

Suddenly, like rapid fire, salmon were shooting through the rapids in a panic. This meant something or someone was coming. Red Bird crouched silently in the tall grasses. His bow was strung and ready. He listened intently, hearing a soft rhythmic splash, splash, splash coming upstream. Emerging from the bend, a huge battle-scarred bear came into view. Red Bird slowed his breath and waited.

Unprovoked, this old bear had recently come into Red Bird's village and attacked a man. Winter was coming, and the village wouldn't be safe while the bear lived. Armed with only a meager bow and his courage, Red Bird waited. He felt his muscles knot in the cold morning air. He willed their release as he watched the bear approach.

He waited until the bear was broadside, swiftly pulled his bow into a full draw, aimed, and shot. The soft thump of the sound of the bow didn't alarm the bear. If the arrow had penetrated, the bear didn't respond. Then, as if his *senses had been aroused, the bear lifted his massive head and looked straight at Red Bird. Slowly and deliberately, he approached the warrior.*

Red Bird, just as deliberately, drew his bow. Knowing that his destiny lay in his next shot, he carefully took aim, looked into the black eyes of the bear . . . and waited. One more step, he thought. One more step and I'll shoot. Suddenly, without warning, the old bear crumpled over. The first arrow had found its mark.

This story of a Native American hunter illustrates that the roots of Red Bird's courage exist far back into the past, to a time long before he had taken his first breath. His prowess as a hunter had its origin long before he was born. His father was a hunter, as his grandfather had been and his great-grandfather. As a young boy Red Bird had learned methods to track and kill prey that were the same methods his father had learned from his father, who had in turn learned them from his father, and so on. The vitally important function of providing food for his family and village was linked to the role of men in his culture for generations.

When people lived in small communities and villages, they often felt a sense of connection to the past that ennobled their acts and instilled a sense of appreciation for those who had passed on the traditions. One man was not just a hunter out on his own, at the mercy of the elements and fate. He was one of a long line of hunters, facing the same difficulties and experiencing the same triumphs as his ancestors. This lineage lent a sense of the sacred to everyday acts and gave a context for interpreting individual experiences.

There was incredible strength to be derived from living in

a world where one didn't feel alone. There was power in knowing that, in addition to being a part of a family and a village, one was also an important link in a long, strong, and unbroken chain, extending backward and forward in time. Questions such as "What is the meaning of it all?" and "Does my life make any kind of difference to anyone?" were very unlikely to arise. It was obvious to each individual what role he played in his culture. It was just as obvious how difficult it would be for everyone if someone suddenly was unable to fulfill his or her function anymore. Everyone depended on everyone else, and everyone depended especially on the wisdom of the elders, because they were the ones who had lived long enough and seen enough to be ready for almost anything.

Carl Jung once wrote: "A human being would certainly not grow to be seventy or eighty years old if this longevity had no meaning for the human species . . . The afternoon of human life must have a significance of its own and cannot be merely a pitiful appendage to life's morning."[1] After one has created a career, perhaps raised a family, and paid dues to society, there must be some purpose to the second half of life.

The elders of ancient cultures were the peace-keepers. Men from their late teens into adulthood often displayed aggressive behavior, but it was the older men, the elders, who abjured aggression, avoided provocations, and encouraged peace. The elders countered the brash tendencies of the young with balance and reason. We have lost this healthy balance.

In addition, in ancient cultures the elders were the guardians of sacred wisdom and inner mysteries. Traditionally, once an individual had completed the childbearing and physically productive years, he or she could then turn his or her energies inward to the spiritual realm. For this reason the spiritual heritage and the legacy of the tribe were laid on the shoulders of the elders for preservation for further generations. The function of the elders as the Keepers of the Memory of the tribe was essential to the survival of the whole society. Without memories a race has no future. For example, the elders may have lived through a great drought that occurred fifty years before. They knew what had to be done in order to survive such a disaster. The lives of the entire community depended upon such knowledge, and the skill and wisdom of these elders.

Recently, I talked to my friend Nundjan Djiridjakin (Ken Colbung) about the place of elders in his culture. Nundjan is the senior male clan leader of the Australian Bibulmun Aboriginal tribe and is actively involved with efforts to preserve and renew Aboriginal cultural practices among the young. He radiates a warmth, strength, and openness, combined with a genuine concern for his people. He said:

In our tradition, the elders were honored because they were the ones who had the knowledge. Long ago there was no written knowledge. We passed on our laws and our knowledge through the oral tradition. And the old people were the keepers of this. They were the ones who had lived longer and experienced more things. They knew what to do if a big storm came or something like that. They were the ones who had the answers. See, it might have been a hundred years since such a big storm or drought had come. And these were the people who had the knowledge in that area. No one else had it. You couldn't just get the information out of a book; you had to get it from one of the old ones. So that's where the respect came in.

Many people feel a lack of connection and meaning in life and subconsciously yearn for the sense of belonging that was an integral part of their ancestors' communities. For some, this need to belong to a group is simply not possible within the context of their own fragmented families. This fact probably accounts for the popularity of cult-type religions and groups that often have strict and very limiting rules governing the behavior of their adherents. One may wonder why anyone would want to belong to such a group, given the large curtailment of personal freedom. It seems likely that members are not so much attracted to the rigid routines and proscriptions as they are willing to endure these restrictions in order to enjoy the sense of belonging to a strong community.

Some of us would never go so far as to join a cult, but we nonetheless continue searching for something that can provide us with that sense of belonging to an ideal that is larger than ourselves. We yearn for something we can believe in and to which we can give our hearts. In addition, we search for mentors, people who have walked before us and who can share their wisdom with us. We yearn for elders. It is as though, on some deep, subconscious level, we need to re-create the experience of belonging to a tribe.

These longings are completely understandable and natural. They are part of our human heritage. Unfortunately, the Industrial Revolution and the incredibly fast pace of change, which is an integral part of modern life, have ruptured the sense of continuity which is our birthright as homo sapiens. When we look at our grandparents and other old people in society, we too frequently find they are not noble individuals who have survived the ravages of time and fate and who hold their wisdom like a precious jewel inside themselves. For the most part our seniors are discouraged people, not unlike us—people who may have become even less wise and powerful at the end of their lives due to their feeling that they are useless and not respected.

We may long to be able to turn to the elders and have them help us find our way. However, the reality of the situation is that in our culture this role has been obliterated over the last century, and as a result, our elderly are no wiser than we are. Perhaps your Great-Aunt May spends every day watching soap operas, and instead of being a revered elder, she has less understanding than you do. This is a tragedy. This problem, which may seem only a small part of the many things obviously wrong with our world, is in actuality quite significant.

The connection with our past, with our ancestors, and with the elders who may still be alive in our families could provide us with a sense of real continuity which could sustain us in our times of doubt and difficulty. However, this link has been shattered by the massive changes occurring in our world. There is a rift, a gaping gash, in the line connecting our past to our future, and we are left lost and longing for something we have no conscious memory of losing.

I believe that re-establishing the sense of connection to our ancestors is a heroic task confronting us at this point in time. It is a task that has been presented to our generation to fulfill. At stake lies not only our personal and familial healing but also the healing of our planet.

The importance of this task is enormous. Nevertheless, we do not need to feel overwhelmed. We may not be able to transform immediately the elders we know into wise ones who can help us find our way; nonetheless there are transformative steps that we can take in this direction. There are actions that we can take now which will have an influential effect not only on our own lives, but also on the lives of those who will follow us.

The simplest and most logical place to start is with yourself. Why? Because you have the most power over yourself. Until you learn to utilize that power fully, you will not be ready to move out into the world with it. Look at your life and where it is heading and imagine yourself in old age. What choices are you making now that will increase your wisdom and power? Is your life of benefit to those who will follow you? What kind of elder will you be? How can you help contribute to our sense of connection to one another?

The fact of the matter is that you are already an elder in many ways, an evolving elder. There are areas in your life where you have learned valuable lessons that have helped you to survive. Take a look at these. Observe them, and then honor the significance they have had in making your own life and the lives of those around you better. No one becomes an elder all at once. Each choice you make, each small victory you achieve in the ongoing process of living, increases your personal store of wisdom and makes you a more valuable member of your community. What made the elders invaluable to our ancestral communities was the vast store of wisdom that they had amassed during their long lives. You are in the process of building that storehouse of knowledge and experience right now. It is a great and highly significant responsibility.

When you live your life with care and a sense of connection to others, you will find that others will turn to you for help and your opinion. This is a sign that you are beginning to function as an elder in the circle of your family, school, church, or whatever you define as your community. We belong to many different circles, some of which overlap. Pay attention to your place in each of these, as well as being aware of the larger pattern of your whole life and what role you can play as an elder.

By choosing to become wise elders, we are actually repairing and re-establishing the continuity of descendance. As we become elders, this begins to restore the path that has been passed down to us from our ancestors. Becoming an elder is a hallowed task that can lend meaning to all aspects of life, from celebrations and victories to times of difficulty and defeat. Asking yourself questions such as "What can I learn from this that could be of value to someone else?" or "How can I explain how I got through this difficult time in a way that is helpful to my grandchildren?" can provide you with a unique and invaluable tool for sorting through your experiences. It can make your everyday actions, even the most mundane ones, significant and sacred.

Once you have made the commitment to become a wise elder, you can begin to honor and cultivate this spark in everyone around you, especially the old ones. All human beings have the potential to be their best self. All of us have the seeds of grace, compassion, wisdom, and love within us. Whatever we expect to occur in life tends to become what we encounter, so when you choose to notice and respond to the nobility in those around you, there is a much greater likelihood that is what you will find in them. Maybe your grandfather is short-tempered and is basically a self-centered man. By believing that he is also capable of so much more, and by knowing that there have been wonderful moments in his life where he exemplified kindness and mercy, you are helping him to become the wise elder that you need him to be. This also helps instill within the vast ocean of collective consciousness the idea of valuing our old ones for their wisdom. And so it will come to be. Small individual acts have a way of gaining momentum until they are mighty, unstoppable movements.

This book contains many different perspectives for approaching the challenge of the coming years. I believe that looking at the long view of our history, extending all the way back into the prehistoric times of our ancestors as well as flowing far into the future, gives us a unique perspective on our lives. This overview of life is a way of perceiving reality that gives us hope and a sense of deep meaning. When you know that you are a vital link connecting your ancestors to your children, then death is not a meaningless tragedy. You know that your spirit lives on. When you die, the legacy that you pass on to your descendants continues to make an essential contribution to their lives. There is the awareness that you are an essential, incredibly valuable part of something bigger than yourself. You know that the actions you take have far-reaching impact because you are connected to everyone around you, those who came before you and those who are not yet born. You experience yourself as a member of the human tribe.

Not everything about our individual and collective past is rosy and nostalgic. It doesn't have to be. Our task is not to deny the negative parts of our past. Part of our destiny is to sort through those behaviors and qualities that have worked well as well as those that have hurt us and kept us from reaching our full potential. That is the meaning of evolution; that is part of the heritage that has been handed down to us.

That is what our ancestors have been doing since they first became human.

Confronted with the enormous challenges facing our world, it is easy to become overwhelmed and filled with despair. However, as we begin to repair the rift separating us from our past, we can also come to realize that all we have to do is take our own small steps in the right direction. That is all our ancestors did. They didn't achieve everything all at once, they took small, individual actions, which collectively made a contribution to the future. In *our* time on earth, we need only do our part and pass on the torch of our best efforts and our highest hopes to the next generation as they pass the torch to those who follow them. This is the power of generations.

2

Finding Your Roots and Honoring Your Ancestors

Several years ago I was given a letter my Cherokee grandmother had written in the 1920s. In it she talked about her turkeys.

> *My years in turkey raising have been both good and lean, but each has been exciting. . . . My ultimate success depends largely on natural factors. For example, this year, saltwater contamination of the creek cost many birds. Coyotes . . . took a very heavy toll, and just when young birds were beginning to roost in the trees, big timber owls came and made off with them in nightly raids. However, there is no more beautiful scene on the farm than my hundreds of turkeys gathering to be fed at sundown in the broad fields bordering the creek timber. Their shiny feathers glow . . . assuring me my hard work has been rewarded.*

As I read her words, written so long ago about her life, I realized that her attitude and even the style of her writing reflected, in some respects, that of my mother, myself, and my daughter. I was intrigued by the similarities that had seemed to ingrain themselves through the generations. For example, in spite of discouragement and so many of her turkeys dying, she found joy in the "shiny feathers."

Reading this passage in her letter, I reflected on how this tendency to see beauty, in spite of difficulty, had penetrated down to her descendants. I recalled an incident from my life when, as a seventeen-year-old, I was shot by a sniper. I was in considerable pain as I was transported from the scene of the attack to a nearby hospital, but as I looked out of the ambulance window, I remember thinking how very lovely the leaves on the tops of the trees looked against the shimmering blue sky. At the time it seemed completely natural to ponder the beauty of the passing trees even though I was wounded. I also thought of how this quality resides in my daughter, Meadow, who was on a soccer team that went three years *without ever making one goal*. Yet after every game she would say, "Mom! Wasn't that great. We really played hard."

I am comforted by the knowledge that a tenacity of spirit and an ability to see the best in people and situations have been passed on to me by my predecessors. A foundation for trust, inner strength, or creativity can come from your family, upbringing, and lineage, but there can also be a darker side to one's heritage. As you trace your roots and find out more about your ancestors, you will find a continuum of characteristics, from the helpful to the harmful, that has come down through the generations to reside in you. The person who you are at this moment is a blending of numerous biological and psychological factors. Part of your sense of self can be traced back to cultural and family conditioning; however, you are also affected by ancestral bequests that can have a powerful effect on your identity, even if you are not consciously aware of them.

PHYSICAL ANCESTRAL BEQUEST: THE PRESENCE OF ANCESTORS IN YOUR GENES

Our ancestors are literally physically a part of us by their presence in our genes. Within each cell in your body is a microscopic trace of every single one of your forebears. It is amazing how, over many generations, facial similarities and other physical resemblances will persist in a family. It is also often noted how psychological profiles or types of mannerisms will be associated with a particular family. Perhaps the men of one family are known for their hot tempers, or maybe many of the women have always married young. It could certainly be argued that some of these traits are due to environmental factors, but the genetic blueprints predisposing familial groups to certain types of behaviors have also been documented. The genetic predisposition to alcoholism is one such cultural phenomenon that has been proved to be present in some genetic populations to a much greater degree than others.

The shamans of Siberia declare that a person can never become a shaman if there have been no shamans in his lineage, because the shamanistic gift passes down from generation to generation through the genes. They believe that not only does the gift of shamanism lie in the blood, but also that ancestors who have been shamans push an individual to follow in their footsteps.

BEHAVIORAL ANCESTRAL BEQUEST

The influence your ancestors have had on your physical appearance may be obvious. Your red hair and the freckles across your nose might look just like Uncle George's, for example. What are more subtle are the hidden values, beliefs, and attitudes that have passed down through the generations. The process of identifying and exploring these hidden attitudes can have tremendous value in terms of gaining a deeper understanding of yourself. While we are all descendants of humanity in general, it is the specific ethnic, biological, and cultural heritages that constitute our backgrounds that make each of us unique.

You are constantly being affected by your heritage, even though these effects might be mostly unconscious or subliminal. Whether you are aware of it or not, your lineage is continually influencing you. Your life destiny is often determined by the things that you aren't consciously aware of or that you choose to ignore. By making a conscious decision to explore the heritage you have received from your family, you can determine which of the qualities you have inherited are enhancing your life and which you would be better off without. This will allow you to become more free to make personal choices about how you live.

When exploring your roots, it's valuable to look for the source of your current behavior. Some of it is learned from your family or is a result of early childhood experiences; other behavior can be attributed to the culture you grew up in, while some is ascribed to past life experiences or can be inherited. Although there are many reasons for your current attitudes and behavior, it is helpful to discover what part of your personality is a result of inherited ancestral patterns. Often, personal choices that we have made might be rooted in familial patterns that have shown up time and time again over many generations. Because many people are not familiar with their ancestors, they may not be aware that choices they have made are part of a larger, repeating family pattern.

My husband, David, was an expert carpenter and worked in the field of home remodeling for more than twenty years before becoming an artist. His work was exquisite and he was, therefore, in demand for restoring beautiful old homes. When his sister became interested in genealogy and researching their ancestors, she found out that many of David's forebears had also been carpenters. David hadn't realized that carpentry was such a part of his heritage. He was particularly interested to learn that his great-grandfather had been employed remodeling homes in Washington State where we currently live. This was not the state David had grown up in, and he was amazed to realize that his ancestor had done exactly the same sort of work he had done in the same state he had chosen to live in.

Laura is a friend of mine who lives in Australia. Recently she decided to research her heritage while visiting England. During her research, she was astonished to find that her father had been raised in an orphanage there. Her father did not like to talk about his past so she was surprised to find out about this aspect of his life. She discovered that the school where he had been raised, the Thomas Coram Foundling School, had been in the Bloomsbury district of London. Even though the school itself had been torn down years before, an education office was still on the original site, so Laura went there to inquire about her father.

A very kind social worker helped Laura with her research into the school records. Additionally, she counseled her about how her father's past might be affecting her emotionally. Laura discovered that her father had been left with a foster wet nurse and later a foster family until he was five years old, at which point he entered the school. After that he saw his foster family only twice a year. The legacy of grief and isolation connected to these events had affected not only Laura's father, but also aspects of her own life. By tracing this information, Laura had much greater insight into her own life patterns and was thus empowered in her ability to change them.

Not only are family traits learned, they may also be inherited. Recent research at the University of Minnesota with identical twins has disclosed remarkable similarities between genetically identical siblings, not only in appearance but in personality, habits, and personal preferences, even when separated at birth. For example, Barbara Herbert, a plump middle-aged woman, found her lost twin, Daphne Goodship, forty years after they had been separated at birth. The coincidences were mind-boggling. They both left school at the age of fourteen, fell down stairs at fifteen, worked in government jobs, met their husbands at sixteen at town hall dances, miscarried in exactly the same month, and both gave birth to two boys and a girl. And this is only the tip of the iceberg regarding the amazing coincidences in the lives of these two women. So it seems that the similarities in twins who are separated at birth may indeed mean that family traits are inherited as well as learned.

Individual qualities are often passed down from one generation to the next without family members being aware that the specific patterns, rituals, and beliefs they are learning are not universal but particular to their own family. In many families, there will be common threads running through choices of profession, personality profiles, ways of approaching problems, and basic life outlooks. These traits will usually be taken for granted by members of the family, who may consider them "just the way things are done" and who, therefore, may be oblivious to the wealth of other choices that exist in other families and cultures. Often they are blind to the existence of their own patterns.

One family might have a perpetual sense of optimism about life. No matter what happens to family members, they always act on a basic belief that things will work out in the end. Another family facing exactly the same kind of events will react to them with a sense of fatalism and interpret every tragedy or difficulty to mean that they are doomed to failure. These basic approaches greatly affect what kind of actions they take and how well they are able to tackle life's inevitable problems. Some family traits and tendencies may be helpful, while others are clearly harmful, but it is only by learning what your own family's heritage is that you will be able to sort out the good from the bad and make choices accordingly.

I recently met a remarkable woman in Sweden named Monica. She and her aunt had done extensive genealogical research, following their family back five hundred years into the 1400s. Monica told me some amazing facts she had discov-

ered about her family. She said that all her direct female forebears (with only one exception) had outlived their husbands
by at least ten years (some as long as almost twenty years) and
had lived into their eighties and nineties, which was highly
unusual in past times. At first she thought she had discovered
a negative family pattern, but on reflection, she realized that
perhaps by outliving their mates the women of her family
had time to develop their spiritual natures without the con-
fines of having to care for the needs of a husband. She also discovered several other ancestral patterns: almost all the women
of her family had difficult relationships with their mothers but
formed real bonds with their grandmothers, and most of the
women of her family had moved from the countries of their
birth.

Although most people cannot trace ancestral patterns
back that far, it is fascinating to see how traits can carry from
generation to generation. We may think that we are teaching
our children only our own values, but in actuality we are both
the recipients and the teachers of a long tradition of characteristics that have made our families the way they are. The
values that we are passing on will extend far beyond our own
lives and the lives of our children. The choices that we make
in our lives are not unique to us. They are actually a distillation of all that has come before us. The more we become
aware of our lineage, the more freedom we will have to honor
what is best and let go of the rest.

A child living with shame learns to be guilty.
A child living with criticism learns to condemn.
A child living with hostility learns to be aggressive.
A child living with domination learns to dominate.

A child living with fear learns to be fearful.
A child living with encouragement learns to be confident.
A child living with praise learns to assure others.
A child living with fairness learns to be just.
A child living with tolerance learns to be fair.
A child living with love learns to love.

DEFINING AND DISCOVERING
YOUR ANCESTORS

In the United States, the two most popular hobbies are gardening and researching one's genealogy. Perhaps the popularity of an ancestral search is related to our need for an understanding of self. The more you learn about your family's ancestry, the more you will learn about your subconscious motives and drives. The more you discover about the forces directing your life, the greater your potential for redirecting your destiny and the destiny of the many generations who will come after you.

There are many valid ways of looking at the notion of ancestry. There are, of course, your biological ancestors, those people whose genes you carry. But if you are adopted or grew up in a family you were not biologically related to, then you will probably consider the family who raised you to be your ancestors as well. There are also ethnic, cultural, and even mythological forebears who have all helped to make up your ancestral heritage and who have exerted a profound influence on how you came to be the person you are. As you explore these influences, your understanding of yourself will increase, and so will your life options.

The Power of Intention in Finding Your Roots

When searching for your family roots, it is valuable to hold the intention that answers will come to you. One of the ways to magnify your intention is through ritual and ceremony. There is great power in symbolic gestures, so you may even want to create a ritual, such as lighting a candle, while you hold the thought that family matters will be revealed to you. The strength of your intention is such that it can activate unseen yet remarkable forces to help you in your search. Even if you are not consciously holding an intention, your subconscious desire to understand and connect with your family roots can put out a silent, yet powerful call to other family members.

I was recently asked to be a commentator on a national television talk show because of my book about signs and coincidences (*The Secret Language of Signs*). Also on the show was a man named John Garcia, who lived in Colorado. One day John was driving down the road and a sudden urge to stop for gas came over him, even though his tank wasn't empty. He pulled into a service station that he had never used before. When he went to pay for the gas, he paid with a check, again something he usually never did when buying gas. The young Eurasian man behind the counter scrutinized the check carefully. Then he asked, "Your name is John Garcia?"

John answered, "Yes."

"Were you ever in Thailand?"

A bit puzzled, John said, "Yes. I was in the military."

The seemingly bizarre series of questions culminated in the man behind the counter asking John if he had fathered a son in Thailand. When John answered in the affirmative, the young man said, "I am your son, Nueng Garcia." It was a remarkable moment. Both men had been wanting to re-establish contact with each other and through an amazing "coincidence," it occurred. It has been a year since their spontaneous reunion and they are now establishing a new relationship. This is an excellent example of how the yearnings of the soul will bring family members together.

Sometimes you may not be conscious of an intention to reunite with relatives, yet loving invisible forces will pull family members together. One spring a number of years ago, my husband, daughter, and I were driving from Seattle to the San Francisco area to attend a wedding. We had decided to do the trip in three days, so my husband and I took turns driving. On extended trips, the non-driver acts as navigator. When I'm the navigator, I tend to ask people for directions. When my husband navigates, he never wants to stop to ask for directions. He is sure that if he looks at the map long enough, he can figure it out.

We got lost driving through the countryside of Oregon, halfway between Seattle and San Francisco. An argument ensued because I wanted to stop and ask directions and my husband was sure he could figure it out without stopping. I was driving, so at the height of our argument, I abruptly turned the car into the driveway of a farmhouse. I turned off the engine, jumped out of the car, and sprinted up to the porch. After a few swift knocks, the door opened . . . and standing before me was my stepsister, whom I hadn't seen in years. We had lost touch with each other, and I did not know where she lived, so our meeting was a complete surprise to both of us. It was a wonderful reunion. We met her children, and our families shared a meal that night. Although I wasn't consciously trying to find her, I believe that I had a subconscious desire to reunite with family members that generated an energy that pulled us together. Since that serendipitous afternoon, we have maintained contact with each other, and I am richer for it.

Biological Ancestors

If you grew up with your biological parents, the easiest place to start your research is with your family of origin. Talk to the living members of your family and ask them what their childhoods were like. Talk to your siblings, too. Their perceptions of your parents and life growing up may be somewhat different from your own and can provide you with an alternative view of your family.

Reunions

Talk to all your living relatives: aunts, uncles, grandparents, cousins, second cousins once removed. A good place to do this is at a family reunion. If your family doesn't have one, you might want to organize one yourself, or perhaps pass on the idea to a particularly social relative. A family reunion is the most natural of settings for retelling old family stories. You might want to take along a tape recorder and a notebook. You can interview older relatives, asking them questions regarding their lives. Find out about the details as well as the overall picture. You might want to ask questions ranging from "What was your first date with your wife like?" to "What would be the title of your memoirs if you set out to write them?" or "What three words would you use to describe yourself?" Getting to know the members of your family in this way will not only be a lot of fun in many cases, but will also provide you with invaluable raw data for looking at family patterns.

Family Tree

Another thing you can do at a family reunion is to start a family tree. Often other family members will share an interest in the history of the family. You might even be lucky enough to have someone in your family who has already made a family tree. You don't have to commit yourself to in-depth family genealogical research in order to construct a simple family tree. Just take a piece of paper and start with yourself and your siblings. Then list your parents and their siblings, parents, grandparents. See how far you can take it back before it gets too complicated or your interest level and/or the information starts to diminish. You might want to assign one page in your notebook for each family member and list on it all the information you can about that person. Of course, you don't have to attend a family reunion in order to get started on this. There are many sources of information for tracing your family's ancestry.

RESEARCHING YOUR ROOTS

The world's largest source for genealogical information is the Family History Library, which is maintained by the Church of Latter-Day Saints in Salt Lake City, Utah. Their records are open to everyone and are the most extensive collection of this kind of information anywhere. There are also many books to help you get started with this, and there are CD-ROM programs especially designed to help you research and construct a family tree. There is also a wealth of genealogical information available on the Internet, ranging from chat rooms to bulletin boards to individual Web sites.

After you have constructed your family tree diagram, you can go to work on your notebook of information about all the members of your family. You can be a detective and find out as much information about each person as you can. This would include basic data such as where they were born, where they lived, whom they married, and when and how they died. However, you will learn much more about your family and yourself if you go further and find out how they were employed, what their hobbies were, what they hoped for and dreamed about, what disappointments and tragedies shaped their lives, what their great triumphs were, and what prejudices they were known to have. You will have to talk to people who knew them well in order to find this kind of information. Other family members, close family friends, old family letters, obituaries, and other newspaper announcements are places to start. You can conduct family interviews over the phone when face-to-face conversations are impossible.

Small pieces of information can yield a wealth of understanding about your forebears. I know of one woman who was having trouble learning about her ancestors because her father had died when she was still young and most of his family were also deceased. She did know that they had lived in the Deep South of the United States since before the American Civil War, although her father's parents had moved to California before he was born.

She also remembered her father telling her a story about having been spanked when he was a boy because he had been whistling a "Yankee" song at home one day. Her father had told her how he had been confused because he didn't know the words to the tune and merely had been whistling it because he thought it was a nice song. From this story, the woman could deduce how much the family had retained old Southern values in her father's generation. She also was able to realize that some of her own values were derived from that culture. Some of them, such as valuing family honor and having a sense of pride about family traditions, were qualities she respected. Other familial qualities, such as racism and discrimination, were ideas that she chose to discard.

Pilgrimage

Making pilgrimages to places where your ancestors lived their lives, where they were born, and where they were buried is an excellent way to connect with your heritage. You can learn about the world your ancestors inhabited as well as how they saw that world. You can sense their relationship to the land they lived on and their place in their community. If no one who knew your relatives is still living there, you can use your intuitive sense to imagine what their world was like for them, and from there you can deduce some of the impact that your forebears may have had on your life.

In your research be sensitive to the meaning of the information you collect. You are looking for the greater context of what it all means, and the living impact that it has had on your life, not just for dead facts. You are trying to find out what kind of people your ancestors were, their idiosyncrasies, their personal traits, what made them unique, not just their biographical data. The more personal and in-depth your understanding of your family's forebears is, the more useful your search will be in understanding your own life.

Do not be concerned about whether or not the informa-

Exercise: Journey Back to
Your Direct Ancestors

This exercise will help you to connect with your biological ancestors. It will introduce you to them so you can begin to understand the forces that have shaped your life and that may have been passed down to you. It can be tape-recorded so you can play it back to yourself, or you can have someone read the exercise to you and act as a guardian while you take your inner journey, or you can embark on this journey from memory.

For this exercise you may want to have some soft, gentle background music, which many people find an aid in visualization exercises. Find a room or somewhere you feel safe from intrusion and where you have some freedom of movement. Stand in the center of the space that you have chosen. Allow your body to feel comfortable and easy. Take a few deep breaths to allow a sense of relaxation to fill you. Take just a moment to be aware of how you feel in your body.

What are the physical and emotional sensations you experience? Just notice and be aware of them without trying to change them. Now imagine that standing directly behind you is your father, if you are a man, or mother, if you are a woman. (This exercise can also be used for an adoptive parent.) Imagine what it would feel like to have this parent standing behind you. Now actually take one step backward, and as you do, imagine that you are stepping into the body of that parent. Take a few moments to adjust to the sensations of being inside that person's body. What emotions and attitudes do you feel? Allow your body to adopt the physical position that best expresses how you feel in that person's body. For example, John stepped backward into his father's image and he felt his body become very stiff and almost rigid. His father had been in the military and used to stand at attention much of the time.

Now imagine that your father's father (your grandfather) is standing directly behind you. Take another step backward, and imagine yourself in his body. Continue this exercise, going backward in time. It doesn't matter if you have no conscious knowledge of your ancestors; just imagine what they could have been like. Each time you step into an ancestor, take a moment to familiarize yourself with him or her. Physically adopt a position for each individual.

Exaggerate and even dramatize the body position until it activates a "knowing" or an intuition about that person's life. This is an important aspect of this exercise. Slumbering in your subconscious mind and in your cells are hidden memories of your ancestors. You can help activate these memories by physically changing your body position to emulate their bodies. Once you have adopted the body position of an ancestor, imagine what the individual's response might be to each of the following questions:

- What is most important to you and why? Career? Family? Health? Possessions? Spiritual growth? Religious affiliations? Hobbies?
- What gives you the greatest joy?
- What gives you the greatest difficulty?

tion you gain from this exercise is factual and historical in nature. The need for everything you experience to be historical fact can block your intuition. If you are constantly acting as your own censor, you block your ability to perceive and receive information. During this exercise, you are attempting to tap into the "ancestral soul," which is the culmination of all the experiences and voices of your ancestors that resound within you. Even if the data you receive is not factually accurate, this exercise is a valuable tool for accessing your intuition, and the information you gain can contain powerful symbols of your inner life and your heritage.

You can do the "Journey Back to Your Direct Ancestors"

exercise again and again, each time tracking a different lineage line. As you do this, notice if there are any commonalities between one line and another. Be aware of similarities in the answers to the questions. Notice if there are likenesses between the mannerisms of certain ancestors and yourself.

Ancestry of Adopted Individuals

If you were adopted and raised by a family who are not your biological ancestors, the tracing of your roots might take a slightly different format. Many people find value in researching *both* their adoptive family's ancestors and their biological ancestors, because they have been affected by both family lineages. However, if you are adopted and feel a stronger sense of connection to the family who raised you than to your biological ancestors, then you can consider your adoptive family's forebears to be your ancestors and your genealogical research can be about them. It may be that the spiritual link to the adopted family is stronger than the biological link, and hence, the adopted family is your true ancestral lineage. But if you always feel like an outsider in your adoptive family or feel a very strong kinship with your birth parents, there can be value in expending effort toward locating your biological parents and finding out as much as possible about them. There are a number of associations that can help you in this process.

If, for one reason or another, you are unable to locate your birth parents, then you can also do the following guided meditation to connect spiritually with them. This meditation can be done even if you do not know anything about your biological family. It can help you connect with your family by tapping into the ancestral information that dwells in the deep recesses of your mind. Just be willing to use your imagination, and this exercise very often allows valuable information to arise from your sixth sense.

Exercise: Guided Meditation
for Adopted Children

In this meditation, imagine that you are in a place where you feel very secure. For some people this might be a lovely place in nature. Others might imagine being at home or in an imaginary sanctuary. Visualize yourself in a number of locations, and then choose the one that makes you feel the safest. Take a while to envision yourself in this location. Picture yourself walking around the place that you have chosen. Make the experience as real as you can. Before meeting your biological family, you may want to imagine having a spirit guardian or angel or loved one by your side. Choose someone who would make you feel very protected and loved. If you have a spirit guardian at your side, take time to talk with that being and feel a sense of connection and safety in its presence.

When you are ready, imagine a magical door through which your biological family can enter into your safe place. They can come through the door one at a time or all at once, according to your

---

desires. It does not matter if some of your biological family are not living anymore; you can still spend time with them. The soul doesn't extinguish when the body ceases to exist. Your ancient biological ancestors may enter through the ancestral door as well. If at any point you feel unsure, you can call upon the assistance of your spirit guardian for support. You have the opportunity to communicate from your heart with each individual who enters through the door. When you feel complete, say good-bye, and imagine each one leaving through the ancestral door.

This exercise is excellent for beginning to heal and resolve family issues from your biological family.

Ethnic Origin Ancestors

Another context for gathering and interpreting information about your ancestors involves exploring your ethnic heritage. There are two ways of approaching this area. The first is to think about the ethnic heritage within which you grew up. For example, perhaps your grandparents were originally from Mexico, but your parents went to great lengths to shield you from feeling any connection to Latin American culture because they felt shame about their parents being poor immigrants in America when they were young. So you were raised in a white, middle-class, suburban neighborhood, where you ate TV dinners and never learned Spanish. Even if this were the case, there may still be a strong need to reconnect with your Mexican cultural heritage because it deeply affected your parents' view of the world, and hence yours, even though they did their best to deny it. This is an example of biological ethnic heritage. In addition to your biological ethnic ancestors, your ancestors are also those who shared your same culture. Although there might not be a direct blood relationship to the ancient members of your grandparents' Mexican village, nevertheless, the individuals in that village can be counted as part of your ancestral pool.

The second way of thinking about ethnic ancestry is to consider the dominant culture you grew up in. For example, if you were originally born in Korea, but you were adopted as a baby by an English family living in London, that is going to have a profound effect on the way you see life, even though you have no biological links to the English culture.

In either case, the ethnic culture that you are tied to, either by biological lineage or cultural environment, may have a far-reaching influence on your life. Even if your ancestral ties go back generations, there can still be an effect on you. For example, if your family has lived in Australia for many generations but originally came from England, or if your family has lived in South Africa for generations but their roots are Dutch, the energy of the country of your family's origin may have an effect on you. Many of the rituals, beliefs, prejudices, strengths, and idiosyncrasies that shape how you live may be linked to the culture you are descended from and/or that surrounded you during your formative years.

RESEARCHING YOUR CULTURAL ANCESTRAL TRADITIONS

Researching the cultural traditions of your ancestors or your childhood family can be both very enjoyable and very revealing. There may be some things you have done all your life that you just take for granted. Maybe you think that everyone does these things, but in fact, they are specifically tied to your ethnic heritage. For example, when I was a little girl, I was not told much about my Native American heritage. And yet I would often go out into the woods by myself for hours at a time and talk to the trees and the earth. I would collect different kinds of plants and roots and call them my "medicine." Later, as an adult, I could see clearly how those behaviors related to my Indian ancestry, even though I had been unaware of it at the time.

Spend some time getting to know the traditions of your family's heritage. Every ethnic group has its own rituals, beliefs, stories, artistic traditions, food, and music. Find out about yours. Read books, talk to old people from your culture, look at the arts and crafts, check out musical recordings from the library, go to an ethnic restaurant, or try out some recipes on your own.

PILGRIMAGE TO DISCOVER YOUR ETHNIC ROOTS

A wonderful way of re-establishing feelings of connection to your ethnic origins is to visit your ethnic homeland. This is a bit different from researching your nuclear family roots. For example, your family may have lived in Canada for eight generations, but your ethnic roots are in Germany. Plan a pilgrimage to the village or city where your ethnic ancestors lived, or if you don't know exactly where they came from, just visit the country or the general area you know was their place of origin. Immerse yourself in the experience of being in the land of your ethnic ancestors. Don't stay in international hotels and eat international food. Stay in little inns or hostels, travel on local trains, take walks through the countryside, and find people you can talk to. You will be amazed at the way this can change your view of the world and the way you see yourself.

Historical Ancestors

Another way of looking at the idea of who your ancestors are is to think about what historical figures had a great impact on your life. These could be individuals whose lives and work greatly affected the person you have become. Are there artists whose views of the world have forever changed how you look at the ordinary objects around you? Has a particular philosopher given you a context for interpreting the key events in your life? Or perhaps you were so impressed by the work of a brilliant scientist that you chose to model your life after his or hers. These people can be considered to be your ancestors also, since the work they did profoundly affected the way that you perceive reality and may have influenced the choices you have made.

Other cultural legacies that might have directly affected your life could have been in the form of important books you have read or music that has spoken to you on such a deep level that your life was never the same afterward. Art, music, literature, folk tales, inventions, new ways of thinking and doing—all these innovations and creations help to shape who we are and how we live. They are part of our cultural ancestry as well, and their influence must be considered as we search for our roots.

Mythical Ancestors

In central Australia, when an Aborigine boy is approaching his teenage years, a special ceremony is held in his honor. His chest is painted with specific designs and he is told that he has been painted with the mark of mythological ancestors of whom he is a living counterpart. This tradition establishes a sense of pride and connection to the greater whole; this rite declares that life on earth is a projection from the mythical and powerful spiritual realms called the Dreamtime. The child himself becomes a mythical infinite being who has incarnated once again; likewise, his friends and companions, during the manhood initiations, also become manifestations of mythical powers from long ago.

Although perhaps not relevant to those living in Western cultures, it is valuable to note that in some native cultures mythic or totem animals are considered to be ancestors. The origins of totem ancestors is not evolutionary. They are thought to be descendants of divine ancestral beings who have taken on symbolic animal form. Totem ancestors are collective beings and are considered sacred. Clan members are divided by their totem ancestors and are connected to the past through the symbolic form of their animal or totem ancestor. If you are descended from a native culture, you may find that totem ancestors play a part in your lineage.

Spiritual Ancestors

Another type of ancestor is the spiritual ancestor who may not be in your direct bloodline, yet nevertheless is your forefather or foremother. A spiritual ancestor can be someone you have known in your lifetime who has passed away but whose impact on your life continues forever. Old teachers, close family members, and friends who were not actually related to you biologically—these people can be your ancestors insofar as they left you a legacy of love and guidance. They, too, helped make you who you are. If you believe in reincarnation, spiritual ancestors can even be those people you have known in past lives who's spiritual legacy continues to have an influence on you.

In addition, some people sense a deep connection with particular spiritual traditions or leaders. Perhaps you feel an affinity for a specific religion, or maybe you do not associate with any actual church, but you always feel profoundly affected by feelings of oneness with nature and the universe. These spiritual connections can provide an unbounded sense of affiliation to things far greater than the self and can be a part of our spiritual ancestry. The sense of union with our spiritual predecessors can provide us with a sense of belonging that transcends limited notions of family, clan, class, or nation. Feeling connected to the source of all creation, which some define as God, lets us know that we truly are all one family; that everyone who has ever lived is our ancestor.

Choosing How to Define Your Ancestors

How you choose to view your ancestors and the context within which you decide to explore your relations can be arbitrary and may change over time. There is no right way to do this. At one point in time you may focus on your actual biological forebears, while at another time you may be more interested in the intellectual forces that have affected your life. Both contexts have validity and great value for helping you discover who you are.

Basically, your ancestors are whomever you choose to identify with. In modern times, the notion of family has had to expand to include divorced and remarried families, families who have relocated to distant corners of the globe, and families who are not tied by any bonds of blood but who have decided to band together into cohesive groups. Discovering the context of how you want to define the term *ancestor* involves a journey of self-discovery, which may first branch one way and then go off in a totally new direction, and yet can be deeply fulfilling and can last a lifetime. The choices that you make in the process both help you to discover who you are and also help to define you at the same time.

Exercise: Ancestors' Circle
Meditation

The following meditation will help you to connect with your ancestors, whether biological, adoptive, cultural, historical, mythical, or spiritual, and invite them to help you in your life. This can be done as a guided meditation. You can either have

---

someone act as your guide and take you through it or you can record this meditation for yourself to play back at a later time.

It is best to do this exercise when you are completely relaxed and have no distractions. You can either lie down or sit, making sure that your spine is straight and that you feel comfortable.

Take a few moments to relax and adjust your body, and then imagine you are walking on a well-worn path across a field. It's a soft, warm, hazy summer day. You are filled with the full, rich smells of the grasses. There is a gentle drone of insects and the sweet soprano of birdsong. These sounds combine to fill the air with a soothing, rhythmic cadence. Ahead of you is a grove of trees. Each tree has a gentle aura of light around it. The path leads you inside this circle of trees. A soft breeze lightly nudges its way through the trees. The leaves moving gently in the wind sound like tiny chimes. In the center of the grove of trees is a circle of large standing stones. Each stone is weatherworn and deeply embedded in the earth. This is the sacred circle of the ancestors. It is a place of power and ancient wisdom.

As you step into the stone circle, you are aware of a soft hum that seems to emanate from the earth. A mist begins to form, first lightly over the ground, and then becoming thicker and thicker.

The mist begins to swirl gently and embrace you with warmth. Though you can't see anything, you can hear the arrival of your ancestors as they come through time and space.

One by one your ancestors appear in front of you. Some people, who are very visually oriented, "see" their ancestors. Other people who are kinesthetic "feel" or have a sense of them being there, even if they can't see them. Some individuals are more auditory oriented, and if you are in that category, then you may "hear" your ancestors speak to you. You may also reach out into the mist and touch your ancestors, and often this allows you to gain a sense of who they might be. It is important to be willing to experiment, and through this you can gain the most distinct experience of your forebears.

As each ancestor steps forward, you have the opportunity to ask questions. You may consider asking:

- What is your life like?
- What is your occupation?
- What are your values?
- What do you believe in?
- What are your skills and talents?

Each of the answers you receive assists the activation of your intuition and offers metaphors for further understanding your heritage.

A very important question to ask is "I am your descendant. What information or wisdom do you want to give me?"

Before each ancestor leaves, ask for and receive his or her blessing. They might give you their blessings in words or in the form of gifts. When you are finished, give thanks for all that has been given, then you can return to normal waking consciousness.

HONORING YOUR ANCESTORS

When a friend heard that I was writing a book that included information about honoring ancestors, she told me she was adamant that she wanted nothing to do with either her family or her ancestors. As far as she was concerned, they were all an extremely negative influence in her life, and she wanted to put as much distance as she could between herself and her predecessors. This is not an uncommon sentiment. Anyone who has suffered a dysfunctional childhood can understand how important it is to distance oneself from family relationships in order to heal. However, even if you feel alienated from your family, you can still gain value from honoring your ancestors; and you can do this without repeating their negative patterns in your life.

To honor your ancestors, you must first forgive them. Forgiveness is important because it helps heal any negative ancestral energy that may dwell in you, such as shame, guilt, anger, fear, hatred, and even denial. The energy surrounding these emotions is so strong that they journey from generation to generation, which is why honoring and forgiving are such important aspects of breaking negative familial patterns (see chapter 3). It is not necessary for you to forgive your ancestors for all their acts, for some acts are unforgivable. However, there can be value in separating the individual from his or her actions, for most deeds are committed as a result of family or ancestral programming. If you can't forgive the deed, then try to forgive the individual. Forgiving and honoring your ancestors helps you to release any negative legacies you may be carrying within yourself and can keep negative family patterns from being passed down to the next generation. So even if you feel that you have inherited a less than exemplary heritage, it is still valuable to honor your forebears.

Our ancestors do not dwell in the past, they dwell inside our brains as well as in every cell of our bodies. By giving our predecessors a place of honor in our hearts, we are acknowledging the gifts that have been given to us by them. No matter what definition you choose to identify your ancestors, finding ways to honor them can empower that place in yourself where your spirit dwells.

Writing an Ancestor Letter

Choose the two ancestors with whom you feel the closest connection and write them each a letter. These letters can be to actual ancestors you have known, e.g., your deceased grandmother, or to someone you have never met, e.g., Mahatma Gandhi, or even to an ancestor you have only imagined. What is important is that you tell them specifically how they have influenced your life and that you thank them for the gifts they have given you.

If you choose to write to real biological ancestors who have now passed on, perhaps you may have some ambivalent feelings about them. Maybe the grandfather who raised you and taught you everything you know about car mechanics was also very harsh with you. It's okay to talk to them about this, too. It isn't necessary to glorify ancestors falsely in order to honor them. On the contrary, acknowledging that they were imperfect human beings, even while they were essential to your becoming who you are, does them even more honor. They faced the problems of their lives as best as they knew how and still were able to pass essential gifts and attributes on to you.

When you have finished writing these letters, you can have a small ceremony in which you burn them and either say prayers or send uplifting thoughts to your ancestors, knowing that the smoke from the fire is taking your prayers and thoughts through time and space to your ancestors on a spiritual plane. Or you may choose to keep the letters and read them from time to time, perhaps even changing parts and rewriting them at some later date when you find that your perceptions have altered.

Honoring Ancestors Through the Use of a Home Altar

Including remembrances of ancestors in a special place in your home is one valuable way of honoring their continuing presence and contributions to your life. Doing this can also function as a remembrance that we are keepers of a sacred trust; that our descendants will inherit what we leave behind us. It can act as a reminder for us to live our lives in a responsible and conscious manner.

In many cultures, a special portion of the home is reserved for an area of sacred space or a home altar. Often this area will be used to honor ancestors. In Japan and other parts of Asia, this space will sometimes occupy an entire room, even with chairs for the departed. Food and incense and flowers are offered there daily to the ancestors. Although it may not be practical to dedicate an entire room of your home as a sacred place, you may want to consider creating a home altar. An altar is a focal point for the sacred, a collection point for bringing together seemingly separate aspects of life into a unified and integrated whole.

Home altars have been in existence for thousands of years, and they come in numerous shapes and sizes. Traditionally, they were a gathering point of power for the home. Having a home altar is like having a small temple in your house; it is a place in the home that is holy. There is great value in setting aside a small area of your home to honor the sacred in your life. The mantel of a fireplace can be made into a lovely shrine, or an altar can be a narrow table put up against a wall, or a round low table. It can be made of wood, glass, metal, or any number of materials and can hang on a wall. A home is more than just bricks, wood, and glass; your home is a focal point for the inter-weaving of many fields of energy. The altar that you create can serve as a constant reminder that all life is sacred. It can function as a center for healing and love and happiness.

You can have an area dedicated to your ancestors on a general home altar, or you can have a special altar dedicated just to the ancestors. An ancestral altar doesn't mean that you are worshiping your ancestors, it is more a reminder of the special place of honor that they hold within your life. An ancestral altar can also be a gathering place for associations and memories and symbols of the past, so that they may be synthesized into your present life. It can help make whole that which has been torn asunder. It is a visible symbol of an invisible reality that marks out part of a unified lineage of humankind.

Your ancestral altar can be as simple as a collection of photos from the past and present (sometimes ancestral altars are created subconsciously when, for example, a collection of family photos is grouped together in an alcove or on the piano), or it can be more elaborate, such as a built-in alcove with special lighting. In addition to favorite photos of your forebears for the altar, you can also have objects that are symbolic of qualities you perceive your ancestors may have embodied. For example, you might place a beautiful stone you picked up on a visit to your grandfather's farm on your altar. The stone will always remind you of your grandfather's strength and steadfastness.

If your ancestors were pilgrims who came to the United States from England and you didn't know any of their exact qualities, you might imagine the fortitude and the inner strength of the convictions that they must have possessed to strike out for a new land in search of religious freedom. To honor their sacrifices and their courage, you might place the feather of a migrating bird that is said to travel great distances in your ancestral sacred place.

You can also put an object on your home altar that has been in your family for a long time, such as the thimble that has been passed down through the women in a family. Alternatively, you can put something that symbolizes your predecessors to you, such as sand if your people were from the desert. To honor special ancestral occasions, anniversaries, or holidays, you might want to burn incense or decorate your home. For example, I heard of a family that lights a candle on the anniversary of the day that Great-Uncle John swam across a freezing cold river to get medical supplies for his pregnant wife.

An altar should be alive with energy, changing and evolving as relationships evolve; one day a fresh spring flower, another day a well-worn river stone can adorn the altar, or another day a single stick of incense and a prayer. You choose the form as the form chooses you. Your ancestral altar can contribute to honoring the past, celebrating the present, and envisioning the future. It can create a powerful metaphor of honoring and uniting with your personal past as well. Including ancestor honor in your sacred space is a way of keeping the trust that our predecessors placed in us, which we will in turn pass on to our children and others whom we love. It is an ancient tradition that deserves reviving.

Calling on Your Ancestors for Help and Guidance

Some cultures utilize the ancestral altar or the ancestral shrine to light incense and ask for help from the ancestors. An exercise that can be of great comfort is to communicate directly with the spirit of an ancestor whom you admire and ask for his or her guidance. This is a very traditional practice in many cultures. Before giving a seminar, I often call on my Cherokee grandmother or on my Cherokee uncle, who are no longer living and who are very important to me, and ask for their assistance. After I have done this, I am always filled with a sense of great calm and confidence.

When my grandmother was living, she was stoic and very stern. She was not the warm and comforting grandmother that I would have liked. At the time she seemed rather cold and distant. After she passed to the other side, however, I could feel her presence, and it seemed that she was changed by the experience. She now was much more gentle and kind, and I experienced her spirit as compassionate and very concerned for me. This is a common phenomenon in cultures that revere their ancestors. The ancestors become fundamentally their best selves once they have passed on.

When you are calling on your ancestors for assistance, you can tell them everything about whatever challenge or problem you are facing. You can remember the courage or the particular qualities you admired about them and ask that they send help in the form of these qualities into your life. This is a particularly powerful form of prayer, and many people have reported dramatic results after they have done this exercise.

Honoring Archetypal Ancestors

Another way to honor your ancestors and invite their presence into your life is by connecting with the Archetypal Ancestors. In many native cultures and ancient traditions, there are rituals for calling on the collective ancestors of the entire tribe or

people. The Maori, for instance, will call upon specific ancestors at one point in their ceremonies, but then they will also
call upon all the ancestors together. In some native traditions,
ancestors are honored as a group or a collective rather than as
specific individuals. In those cultures, when they call upon the
ancestors, they call upon the archetypal forebears that possess
the ancestral soul that dwells in all their predecessors.

Archetypal Ancestors encompass the collective wisdom
and power of all those who have preceded you. In Western
culture, many folk tales contain this archetype in the form of
the Wise Old Woman or the Wise Old Man. This image is a
universal one. You might consider embarking on a meditation
to help you find and connect with your Archetypal Ancestors.
One visualization technique you could employ is to imagine
that you are at the base of a mountain. There is a pathway
leading up this mountain, and you know that this path will
take you to your Archetypal Ancestors. All the wisdom,
strength, courage, and power that have ever existed in your
family lineage are exemplified in these individuals. Imagine
journeying up to the top of the mountain and taking time to
communicate with these beings. When you are finished, you
are given a gift by the Wise Woman and/or the Wise Man,
which you carry down the mountain with you. Anytime you
think of this gift, you open the channel to the inner wise
woman or wise man who dwells within you.

*You follow in the steps of the ancient ones who have gone
beyond you. In no small way everyone and everything that has ever
existed is your ancestor. Your cells contain the blueprint of all life
and all form and all being. Your ancestors dwell within you. Honor
them and you honor the sanctity and sacredness that dwells within
all life, within you, and within the cosmos.*

3

Breaking Free from Negative Ancestral and Family Patterns

Your past is not gone. It is here now. It is still happening. To be alive is to have a past. Your psyche has not arisen from the present; its source goes back thousands of years. It is only a new sprout from an ancient root. Although it is common to think that attitudes and beliefs are self-generated, much of your personality and consciousness has sprung from the deep and primordial ancestral legacy that dwells within you. The formation of your identity is, in part, the result of the progressive lineage of your predecessors. The way you experience life is filtered through the experiences of all the generations who preceded you. Your sense of self rests strongly on the experiences you had as a child, and those experiences, in large part, were created by your family, who in turn were influenced by their childhood families and so on back through time. From this heritage you have gained positive qualities that strengthen and empower you, but qualities such as distrust, fear, and isolation may also be a part of your legacy.

The vast range of negative human emotions, such as frustration, anger, and fear, felt throughout history can be subliminally recognized in ourselves as our "human nature." Though some people have romantic visions of ancestors, human nature hasn't changed much through the centuries. Your ancestors probably experienced jealousy, resentment, rage, and sorrow as much as anyone who lives in the present time. They probably repeated the same patterns, both negative and positive, as their parents, grandparents, and beyond. Physical traits, and even some psychological tendencies, such as schizophrenia, are genetically bestowed from one generation to the next. In addition, behavioral inclinations, such as sexual abuse, incest, and dysfunctional attitudes, can be traced back through family history. Sometimes habitual ancestral patterns and traits resurface again and again throughout generations in an almost mystical manner. It's as if a deep aquifer of ancestral consciousness—an ancestral soul—flows underground for several generations, and then resurfaces, tapping into the consciousness of present-day descendants.

The ancestral soul can have such a penetrating effect on the psyche that it can even influence one's destiny. It is especially interesting to note this tendency in some adoptees, who, as adults, trace their biological roots and discover an uncanny number of similarities between themselves and their far ancestors. Adopted at birth, these individuals would have had no conscious way of being programmed toward the particular professions, attributes, and traits they share with their ancestors, yet this phenomenon of ancestral similarities can be documented again and again. It is not uncommon in the Aborigine tribes of Australia for young men, who have been raised without knowledge or exposure to the traditions of their ancestors, spontaneously to paint themselves in the traditional style of their ancestors. Nundjan Djiridjakin, a tribal elder of the Bibulmun Aboriginal tribe in Australia, told me an interesting story about how ancestral traditions are being renewed by young people who have never been taught these traditions:

> *The spirits of the old people who have gone are coming back through the young. We recognize this by the fact that some of the young have been producing drawings and paintings that they have never been taught. It seems that they carry the knowledge that is necessary to do the strokes for this traditional form of body painting in their subconscious. We believe that this is evidence that the ancestors are still with us and that they are still in control of our destiny.*

Our genes are encoded with the imprints of our ancestors, so perhaps ancestral memories or the ancestral soul also dwell in our genes. This phenomenon may be apparent in twins or siblings who, although separated at birth, still somehow cultivate the same interests and display the same mannerisms. I once met twins who were separated at birth and were brought together years later by remarkable coincidences. They found themselves attending the same college in Canada and had a number of mannerisms in common. They found that they shared remarkable similarities; such as both men were twenty-five years old yet neither of them had a driver's license and both had an avid passion for chess. I also met two sisters who had been separated at birth who, again through remarkable circumstances, found themselves working in the same department store. They had even unwittingly become friends. They both left school at sixteen and married older men. Whether the life similarities in siblings separated at birth can be accounted for by an ancestral soul or genetic encoding, the end result is the same. We are all influenced by our relations, even if we are not consciously aware of them.

Your ancestry and your genes are affecting you at every moment. Sometimes we are affected positively by the past, but sometimes the weight of the ancestral soul has a negative influence on our lives. The legacies from our predecessors can have a staggering effect on our emotions, especially if they are not examined. The ancestral soul is ever present within you, in one form or another, ever ready to be re-actualized. Denial or refusal of your roots often creates a polarization, so that, in effect, you are still programmed by your past. The past is what makes the present coherent, and it will remain damaging for as long as we refuse to examine it honestly.

You do not have a choice about having a past. Your past is a given. You do have a choice whether you will repress, explore, or re-create your past. You can either fight with the unresolved past that dwells inside you, or you can examine the forces that shaped it and even reshape it. Modern therapy initiates psychological healing by unearthing memories from childhood and early family relationships. However, many negative patterns have their source beyond early childhood. Conventional therapy can deal with most difficulties, but problems that don't seem resolvable through traditional means might be resolved by tracking into the far past. Breaking free from negative ancestral patterns or ancestral unfinished business can heal the family tree.

HEALING THE FAMILY TREE

I've created a four-step program I call Healing the Family Tree. The first step in this program is to remember and uncover memories from the past, both personal and ancestral. The second step involves discovery and identification of negative or dysfunctional familial tendencies. The third step is to break free of these patterns so that they don't go beyond you. The fourth and last step is to create new patterns that become your legacy to the future.

1. Remembering and Uncovering

We are called to repeat that which we cannot remember. The patterns of the past loop and fold back on themselves in a compulsive, repetitive manner. That is what we call karma. Our lives are determined by the past, particularly the past that is forgotten. The experiences of the past still can cast long shadows that can darken the future.

One of the longest shadows that can darken your life is created by family secrets and lies. They are destructive because they are almost always based on shame and guilt, which weaves its way into the family psyche. Lies build on lies, and the stress of bottling up secrets takes an enormous psychological toll on families. The lies needed to sustain family secrets become transmitted across generations. The psychic energy from family secrets weighs heavily on an entire lineage.

Secrets can take on a life of their own. They can create "territories of the unspoken," where there are tacit rules that those subjects can never be discussed. Often there will be some family members who know the secret and some who do not. This division creates covert alliances to keep the secret. Those who don't consciously know of the secret are still deeply affected by its negative influence on their psyches. For example, a child who doesn't consciously know the secret will often begin to metaphorically act out the same behavior that underlies the secret. Children know and feel the unspoken; they have an inner radar for the forbidden, dark secrets of a family. They might begin seemingly "inventing" stories and telling lies, but often beneath this behavior are serious family issues that are not being expressed.[1]

A child who grows up with family lies will often carry that behavior into adulthood. For example, a mother brought her fifteen-year-old son, Kevin, to a New York family therapist. The mother was upset because the child had been stealing money from the family and was failing at school. The therapist was astute enough to realize that there was a lie somewhere in the family system. Eventually, through research, it was discovered that Kevin's great-grandmother (whom he didn't know) was a petty thief and also had a reputation for lying, *but her actions were never discussed by the family.* It is more often the unspoken and unseen that rule our destiny than what is known and discussed. Kevin's mother perpetuated this family circle of lying by covering up the truth that Kevin's father was an alcoholic and a drug dealer. She rationalized her actions by believing that if she told Kevin the truth, he might follow in the footsteps of his father. The therapist suggested that Kevin's lying had its roots in the family tradition of secrecy and denial. Through deep and candid communication about family issues, Kevin's behavior dramatically improved within a year.[2]

Many families have secrets centered around adoption and

parentage. Research has shown that rather than being protected by not knowing the truth about their parentage, children experience a devastating sense of betrayal when they find out the truth (and they usually do). And even if they never discover the truth, the off-limits areas in the family and the hundreds of lies used to cover up the truth have been shown to have a negative effect on individuals over time.[3]

It's not uncommon for virulent secrets to skip a generation or so before plaguing the descendants, so take a hard look at any family secrets you may be harboring. To heal the family tree, it is important to remember and learn what you can. To recall your personal memories, as well as the ancestral memories that dwell within you, there are several things you can do.

PERSONAL MEMORIES

Going back into personal childhood memories can help you understand the forces that shaped you. The past experiences that continue to motivate us aren't usually the ones that we can consciously recollect in great detail but those that have slipped below the surface of the conscious mind. The exercise below can help you remember your past.

• Start by going backward in time. Obtain a journal, and use at least one page of paper for every year of your life. Write as much as you can about the experiences of that year that you remember. Don't be concerned if you don't remember anything for parts of your life. One recovered memory will often inspire memories from another time. Also, detail stimulates your memories, so recall as many details as you can.

• Draw a floor plan of your childhood home or homes. It's

often difficult to separate who we are from where we are. Close your eyes, and imagine that you are exploring each room. We often associate memories with locations, and exploring your childhood house, room by room, may stimulate memories for you. During your exploration, notice the emotions and feelings that each room elicits in you. Even if the memories are still buried, the emotions you feel may offer clues to those forgotten experiences from the past. Pay special attention to the rooms that you are reluctant to enter.

• Repeat the above exercise imagining yourself in your neighborhood, friends' house, homes of relatives, your hometown, and on shopping trips, vacations, and so on. Try to recall as much detail as you can from each place, paying special attention to the feelings associated with each location.

• Your sense of self has also been shaped by the organizations and corporations you have been a part of. These corporate bodies have contributed to your beliefs and attitudes. Locate memories of yourself in churches, schools, businesses, organizations, and athletic teams. List these in your journal.

ANCESTRAL MEMORIES

Remembering ancestral memories can be valuable in your recovery process. You may think, "How can I remember someone else's memories?" The process is actually easier than you think. You are uncovering the ancestral memories that dwell inside you. When a chick first pecks its way out of the shell, it will cower if it sees the shadow of a hawk flying overhead. It doesn't do this if a robin or pigeon flies overhead. It has a residual memory of the dangerous nature of hawks. You could say that it has an ancestral memory of hawks eating chickens in its unconscious mind. You also have ancestral memories residing deep within you; this exercise will help you recover some of them.

- Close your eyes and imagine a long table with masks on it. Each mask looks like and represents one of your ancestors. (This includes your most recent ancestors—your parents, aunts and uncles, grandparents, great-grandparents—as well as your ancient ancestors.) Every mask has magical powers. When you put on a mask, you experience the feelings, thoughts, and experiences of the person it represents. Begin putting on different masks to experience the viewpoints of your ancestors. Pay particular attention to the masks that you feel very uncomfortable wearing. Don't worry whether what you are experiencing is accurate or not. Even if the images you see and the emotions you feel are not completely accurate, they nevertheless represent important communications from your subconscious mind and they deserve to be heard.

- If you have any objects that belonged to your ancestors, hold each object, one at a time, and imagine that your body metamorphoses into the form of the ancestor who owned the object. The article might be a piece of jewelry, an antique, a ceremonial object, a souvenir, or a tool. Different aspects of people's lives are recorded in the objects they have left for their descendants. Notice your mental, emotional, and physical sensations. If you find yourself saying, "But I don't know what they felt," you can make the following statement to yourself: "I don't know, but *if* I did, what would it be?" This very simple sentence makes it easy to slip around the logical mind and reach into your inner knowing.

I own a turkey feather that belonged to my Cherokee grandmother who raised turkeys. It is over fifty years old, and it is one of my cherished possessions. I used the feather to embark on an inner journey to visit the world of my grandmother. As I held the feather, I began to imagine what my grandmother must have felt when she held it. I could sense her immense pride in her turkeys. Continuing to hold the feather, I felt myself dissolve as my identity began to merge with my grandmother's. It was as if I were seeing the world through her eyes. I almost felt that, for a short while, I became her. I could feel a sense of reward for the time and energy she spent with the turkeys. I could feel her patient strength fill me. I could also feel her sadness and longing. It was as if I could hear her thoughts: "There is always so much work to do. I take pride in my work, yet sometimes it seems that I would like time just to be with my children without always working."

When I came out of my meditation, I experienced an infinite compassion for my grandmother. I understood aspects of her that had been previously unrevealed. I also recognized in myself a similar pattern of always being busy and not taking time off to relax. Perhaps my constant busyness was part of my grandmother's legacy to me. Knowing that my pattern of busyness may have had its source in my ancestral past helped me to understand and begin to change it.

2. Identification of Negative Ancestral Patterns

The second step in Healing the Family Tree involves doing an honest and thorough self-evaluation. In this discovery process, it is valuable to spend time identifying what your beliefs are regarding yourself and your life, especially beliefs that have been handed down to you. A belief is a thought or a perception that you consider to be a fact or a reality, and it can be a direct result of the emotional and psychic legacy of your family and ancestors. Beliefs are very powerful and can determine the way you think and behave. In fact, they can literally determine the course of your life. Discovering *your* beliefs can help you uncover the belief systems that have passed down to you through your predecessors and can help prevent you from passing negative beliefs to your descendants.

In order to understand the familial beliefs that have descended to you, it helps to comprehend the underlying dynamics of how beliefs work. Your beliefs can dictate the quality of your life, and the most powerful of your beliefs are your subconscious ones. These are generally so deep-seated that you're not usually aware of them. Even if you were not explicitly told of your parents' beliefs, they were nevertheless communicated to you. As a child you watched your parents' faces and body language to see how they responded to particular situations. Your connection to them meant that their opinions and beliefs were very important to you.

Nancy's experience is an example of how beliefs are passed down through family members. She consciously thought that she trusted men, but on a subconscious level, she believed that they could not be trusted. Although she was not told this in so many words, nevertheless this belief was passed down from her mother through her expressions and reactions to particular situations. Her mother in turn had learned it from her mother, who had learned it from her mother, and so on. Because of this familial belief, women in this lineage chose men who could not be trusted, because what is expected tends to be realized, thus perpetuating this belief from one generation to the next.

Beliefs affect your perception of reality just as tinted glasses allow only certain colors to reach your eyes. Subconscious programming comes from the ancestral soul, from the way others related to you when you were a child, from decisions made in your present life and in past lives, as well as from the collective unconscious of the society in which you live. These beliefs can become so deeply embedded in your mind that they constitute part of your "ground of being." Beliefs that are part of your ground of being do not seem as if they are based on individual decisions or perceptions; they are those assumptions that you take to be truth, or simply "the way it is." This can be likened to the air you breathe. Oxygen is so much a part of our ground of being that we don't have conscious awareness of it surrounding us at all times. Air is such a fundamental part of what we take for granted as "reality" that we almost never think about it.

Beliefs that become embedded in our psychological make-up act as magnets, attracting situations and people that are congruous with those subconscious beliefs. This means that your personal world is constantly created by the beliefs that exist in your subconscious mind. If you are not sure what your subconscious beliefs are, just look at your life. Your life is a projection of your inner beliefs about yourself and life. It is valuable to discover your beliefs, especially the ones that have descended from your ancestors, because then you can separate negative beliefs from helpful ones, and, consequently, you won't pass the damaging traits down to your descendants.

Very likely your ancestors shaped many of the beliefs that you hold. Strong negative attitudes have a tendency to reinforce themselves and are, therefore, difficult to dilute through the generations. Vengeance, fear, rage, guilt, and shame are difficult to erase from the ancestral soul. By tracing the roots of each of your beliefs to its source, you can begin to heal negative ancestral attitudes that are creating difficulties in your life.

To begin your discovery process, make a list of your beliefs. A belief can originate from your life experiences, your family upbringing, the culture you live in, your ethnic background, your past lives, or even the collective unconscious. Not all beliefs can be traced to your ancestors, so examine each one to see if it may have been passed down through the generations. After each belief, list all the places where it might have originated.

---

*Exercise: Examining the
Origins of Your Beliefs*

EXAMPLE:

BELIEF: Only people with a lack of control show their feelings.

ORIGIN: Family and ancestral. When Al was a child, he was punished for showing his feelings. He was told a man needs to be strong and not cry. His father didn't show his feelings. His grandfather and his great grandfather didn't show their feelings.

---

*Exercise: Examining the
Origins of Your Beliefs*

EXAMPLE:

BELIEF: It is important to work hard.

ORIGIN: Family, ancestral, cultural, and ethnic. Ty's
family lived in Minnesota. They were first-
generation Germans living in a community with
many other Germans. Ty's belief about hard work
was instilled in him by his family when he was a
young boy. He knew that this belief was also shared
by his ancestors. In addition, the overall belief in
that particular German community was toward a
very strong work ethic, so this would show a
cultural origin in his belief. He felt that his belief
may also have had an ethnic origin, because there
is a stereotype that Germans are hardworking.

During your discovery period, research your roots and
genealogy to track down family traits and attitudes. Talk to
relatives to retrieve family history. Be patient but persistent.
Find out as much as you can about the psychological and
mental make-up of your ancestors. Sometimes you may feel
uncomfortable when researching family history and patterns,
since you may encounter negative traits and may end up
bringing some family skeletons out of the closet; however, it is

essential that you are stalwart and go clear to the heart of the matter. Mary Gordon, a well-established Catholic novelist, decided to write a biography of her father, who died when she was seven years old. She was distraught to find out that her idealized father was actually an anti-Semite who had lied about his career. Remember, you are tracing your roots not just for yourself but to heal the family tree for the generations that will follow you. The burden of unfinished ancestral business can be lightened only by: first, becoming aware that it exists; second, acknowledging (not blaming) ancestral shortcomings; and last, being willing to address the problem and actively pursue a release to truly initiate the healing process.

3. Breaking Free from Negative Ancestral and Family Patterns

When we encounter a negative ancestral belief, it is vital that we say through both our words and actions, "The buck stops here!" Declare to yourself and the world at large, "This is the last generation that this negative pattern will affect. I'm making a stand for myself and those who follow me. I'm breaking the negative ancestral cycle and replacing it with a new one." The longer the cycle continues, the more deeply it engraves itself into the psyche of our family lineage. And if you don't stop the cycle now, you may unwittingly pass it down to your descendants.

There is a particular trait unique to human beings that makes it difficult to break an ancestral cycle. We are the only creatures on the planet that declare, "I'm right and you're wrong!" We are the only species that holds on to beliefs and attitudes long after they have outgrown their usefulness. In the natural process of evolution, traits that are necessary for survival are retained and passed on, while those that don't have this value are left behind. However, humans will hold on to a belief or attitude, even if it is destructive, long after it is no longer appropriate. I believe that this phenomenon occurs because human beings have a desperate need to be "right." The man who says, "I'll show you!" and kills himself is a prime example of someone who wants to hold on to his point of view so tenaciously that he is willing to die for it. If a human being believes, for example, that another race of human beings is inferior, he may hold on to this belief, no matter what the evidence is, in order to be "right" about his beliefs.

BREAKING A NEGATIVE PATTERN THROUGH AN ACT OF WILL

In order to begin to break the cycle of negative beliefs, you will have to relinquish the need always to be "right." This can be extraordinarily difficult. It is an act of power to release a deeply held belief through conscious decision. It is an exercise in using your will, which is a divine path to change. For example, Jim came from a family that always seemed to be victimized by people and circumstances. As he explored his heritage and upbringing, he saw that he had accepted his family's attitude and often found himself a victim of circumstances. One day Jim garnered his inner strength and declared to himself, "I'm no longer a victim of life. I accept responsibility for myself. I always have choices in my life. Although I may not be able to choose my life circumstances, I can always choose the way I respond to the events in my life. I declare this for now and for always." Jim found that his declaration gave him a sense of inner power that allowed him to begin to release an age-old family pattern.

There is power in your intent and your words. After you become aware of a negative ancestral pattern, be willing to make a stand. It's as if you are standing high on a mountain that reaches into the heavens and, with your fist raised, you declare, with passion and power, "This pattern stops here!" The past loses its hold over you once you become aware of its role in your life. You are in charge of your life now. It is time to stop blaming the past for your life today. Your parents did the best they could, given their upbringing. Their parents did the best they could, given their upbringing. Acknowledge the events and patterns of your past—and then get on with your life.

BREAKING FREE OF DEEPLY INGRAINED FAMILIAL PATTERNS

An "act of will" can help free you from negative patterns. It can be a powerful step toward liberation from old programming. It can be the touchstone that changes an old pattern forever. However, sometimes familial patterns are so destructive and so deeply ingrained in the psyche that it takes more than an act of will to release them. In these cases, therapy is recommended to ferret out the origins of the limiting beliefs from childhood and from the ancestral soul that dwell within you. In therapy there are several stages that you may go through in your healing process. Because healing is a highly individual process, you may not always pass through these stages in order. You may even go through the same stages again and again, but each time you will heal from a different vantage point.

BREAKING-FREE STAGES:

1. Deciding to Heal

The first stage is making the choice to heal. Often this is where an act of will is valuable. State to yourself, "I am ready and open to heal." With these words you have initiated the healing process. The first step in any healing is the willingness to heal.

2. Turmoil

After the initial decision, there is often a period of turmoil. Although this stage can be uncomfortable, this is actually a very good period. It is now that memories from the past—from childhood or even ancestral or past-life memories—may begin to surface. Memories will often surface in dreams. They can also come in spontaneous flashes of memory during the normal activities of life.

During the turmoil stage, you may feel anger or grief about the aspects of your life that the familial patterns wounded. You may even feel self-righteous and have no compassion for those who have handed you a familial pattern. These emotions are valuable because they are a way to honor your pain so it can be released. Often the impact of a family pattern is so deep and painful that we bury those experiences deep inside ourselves until they are denied or even forgotten. In order to heal, it is valuable to remember what happened and take time to experience and express your emotions.

It is also during the turmoil stage that the pattern that you want to release can seem to become even stronger, almost as if it has a consciousness of its own and is striving for survival. In fact, this stage can be likened to the lancing of a wound.

Although a lanced wound may look worse, the process actually brings toxic material to the surface so that it can be released.

For example, Ben was a very angry individual. His father was also very angry. In exploring his family patterns, Ben was able to trace the obstinate family anger back several generations, so he realized that his anger was part of an inter-generational family problem. After he made the decision to heal the anger, he noticed that his anger was actually increasing, which made him very distraught. Instead of being less angry, he found himself becoming enraged more frequently. When he became aware that the decision to heal can sometimes activate a familial pattern, he was able to see why so much anger was emerging. This awareness allowed Ben to enter into the next stage of the healing process.

3. Understanding the Past

The next step is to move toward understanding. Understanding the subliminal motivations of others and yourself assists the healing process. It's also important to realize that negative familial patterns aren't your fault. Children tend to think that the negative circumstances of their lives are their faults. An abused child often thinks he or she deserved the abuse. You are not to blame for the negative patterns in your life. It may be true, from a spiritual perspective, that we generate the circumstances of our lives to learn and to grow; however, there is no value in feeling blame or guilt.

Healing can occur from understanding that everything that has occurred in your life has allowed you to learn and to grow *but was not your fault.* You were acting on programming from your past, and those who emotionally injured you were acting on programming from their past, and so on. When you begin to understand the dynamics of why you are the way you are and why others have treated you the way they have, the way is paved for healing.

4. Resolution

This is the stage where you come to a resolution with who you are. You can't erase your family history, but you can make lasting changes in your life so that familial patterns don't repeat into the future. You develop a compassion for those who have gone before you and reach a point of integration within yourself, which helps you contribute to making a better world. Find a way to make peace with actions that have had a negative impact on your life. Perhaps you can never forgive, but it is important to deal with family patterns in some way that doesn't damage you emotionally. It's all right to hold people accountable for their acts. It's all right to feel angry. You do not need to forgive to come to a resolution. Resolution is acknowledging that you have been negatively affected by a family pattern; you might not have released it from your life, but you understand it and you have survived. With compassion and humor, you accept who you are and where you are in your inward journey toward healing.

Sometimes during the resolution period, you can restructure the story of your past (see chapter 5). Look over your personal story, and notice if you were rewarded for being a martyr. Did you get attention for being sick? Did you gain a sense of mobility for striving without ever succeeding? What did you gain from being a victim? Victims are helped when they say "I can't" and punished if they say "I won't." As a culture, we assume the valiant nature of the victim; however, could it be that the meek inherit the earth because they deplete the life force of the courageous and the brave? Restructure your story. Even if we are truly victims of life and are not responsible for our experiences, adopting the viewpoint that one does carry some responsibility is remarkably empowering. As an exercise, rewrite your story in such a way that the reader would laugh at your foibles instead of pitying you.

5. Forgiveness

After you have found resolution with your family patterns, the last step is forgiveness. This is perhaps the most important stage. It helps you release energy that has been diminished by harboring anger, bitterness, and resentment. Forgiveness can allow you to get on with your life rather than nursing old wounds. It is human to want to punish, with your anger and bitterness, those who have wronged you, but no amount of punishing those who hurt you will help heal you. In fact, the anger that you hold on to damages *you*, not them. Forgiveness is something that you do for you; it is for *your* sake and for *your* healing that you forgive. You forgive to gain inner peace, joy, and serenity for yourself, not necessarily for the people who wronged you.

Some people hold on to their resentment because they have a subconscious belief that sooner or later their nemesis will apologize or "make it up to them." If they haven't by now, they probably never will. You may never be able to "even the score." Those who wronged you may never change, and even if they did, would it really alleviate your pain over the injustice that you have suffered? Others hold on to resentment and hatred as a justification for continuing to act like a victim in life. Their being wronged becomes their excuse for not living the lives they desire and for everything that is wrong with their lives. Forgiveness means being willing to grab life by the reins and let go of being a victim of life's circumstances.

The first step of forgiveness is understanding the inner motivations for the acts of others and yourself. However, forgiveness doesn't mean that you need to forget, absolve, or condone the actions of another. You may never be able to forget or forgive the *deeds*, but there is tremendous value in forgiving the individual who committed the deeds. This applies to yourself for your deeds as well. Understanding that each person's actions are dictated by his or her conditioning makes it easier to forgive.

All human beings, in every instant of their lives, have done the best they knew at that particular point in time. Even if, in retrospect, they could see other possibilities, in the moment, they responded as well as they could given their early childhood conditioning, ancestral programming, and the influence of their culture. It is valuable to understand why people act the way they do, and it is also helpful to acknowledge the reality of who those people are now. This means that an individual may have the capacity to commit hurtful acts again. Forgiveness doesn't mean that you need to become that person's best friend. Understanding why an individual acts the way he or she does and acknowledging the truth of the situation can be enough to begin a healing process.

Forgiveness can be extremely difficult. *True forgiveness is usually an ongoing process: it is not a one-time absolute decision. It isn't an act; it is a context.* Forgiving can't be forced. It isn't as easy as blithely deciding, "Okay. Right now, I'm forgiving that person who harmed me." Making a unilateral declaration of forgiveness usually doesn't work; neither does listing everyone you want to forgive, and then ticking off each name as you try to forgive them one by one. It just doesn't happen that way. Forgiveness usually comes as a result of honestly exploring the past and your roots, and then gaining understanding of the forces at play in the situation.

Forgiving can take time. It takes as long as it takes, and it's important to have patience with yourself and your internal process. There may be some days when you feel completely free of past resentments, and there may be days when they seem to well up again. Sometimes forgiveness can be a way of negating your anger before you are ready to release it. It's important to honor the process and allow yourself to be where you are, while at the same time holding an intention for forgiveness to occur.

Sometimes forgiveness can be interactive. Talking with family members for whom you harbor bitterness can sometimes be helpful. But not everyone is receptive to communication, and sometimes the initial attempts to communicate are extremely difficult and don't meet your expectations. If you speak from your heart and your truth, your words might be seeds that take root at a later time or even in later generations. When you are not able to heal through communication, or if the person with whom you are angry is dead, it is valuable to reach into the inner realms to find resolve and peace (see the exercise below for acceptance of ancestors). When you truly cross the threshold to forgiveness, you break the cycle of negative patterns of abuse, ridicule, betrayal, rejection, discouragement, cruelty, abandonment, lack of love, failure, or scorn that have continued generation after generation. You initiate a new cycle of love, support, and kindness that will follow you for generations to come.

Exercise: Comparing Your Attitude with Your Ancestor's Attitudes

EXAMPLE:

	Work	Relationships	Sex
Sue's attitude	workaholic	shy	fearful
Mom	workaholic	withdrawn	unsure
Dad	pragmatic	outgoing	relaxed
Uncle Harry	balanced	outgoing	womanizer
Aunt Maud	workaholic	formal	unsure
Grandmother Doris	idle	formal	bored

EVALUATION EXERCISES TO BREAK NEGATIVE PATTERNS

In order to break negative ancestral patterns, it is important first to establish what those negative patterns are. One way to do this is to examine the attitudes of your predecessors toward different aspects of their lives, and then compare these with your attitudes. For example, Sue compared her unwillingness to say what she really felt with a discovered pattern that most of the women in her family lineage had been very afraid to speak their minds. To help you discover and compare attributes, it is helpful to make a chart with a list of your family members and ancestors. The next step is to do the following Ancestor Evaluation Exercises and fill in the spaces of your chart accordingly. When your chart is complete, you can see if there are any similarities that have passed down through the generations to you.

Money	Health	Religion	Creativity	Food
needy	poor eyesight	none	sewing	unimportant
restrictive	heart	none	afraid to try	unimportant
generous	good	none	woodwork	enjoys
relaxed	gout	none	stamps	enjoys
anxious	arthritis	none	painting	unimportant
uninterested	arthritis	Baptist	collecting	picky

(When constructing your list, record both the ancestors you are consciously aware of and the ones you contacted through visualization and imagery. See chapter 2, "Finding Your Roots and Honoring Your Ancestors.")

Evaluation Exercise 1

Our attitude toward career and work is often a reflection of the work ethic of our immediate family and our ancestors. Here are some adjectives that describe work and career attitudes:

adventuresome, ruthless, motivated, timid, lazy, head-strong, hard-working, passive, obedient, ambitious, honest, dutiful, productive, inconsistent, loyal, good at starting but not finishing, not good at starting or finishing but good at maintaining, good at finishing but not starting, dishonest, workaholic, dynamic, put things off to the last

minute, organized, lackadaisical, disorganized, follower,
leader, fearful, bored, determined, idle, take-charge, erratic

1. Find the words from the list above that best describe
what *you perceive* your ancestors' attitudes to their careers to
be. Put the qualities on your chart.

2. Which of the words describe your attitude to work?
Write those qualities on your chart. Note if there is a similarity between your list of qualities and your ancestral list of
qualities.

3. If there are positive qualities that you share with your
ancestors, it is valuable to acknowledge and honor the ancestors (see chapter 2) who may have helped contribute to those
attributes.

4. If there are negative attributes that you share with your
generational family, look to see what action you can take to
begin to de-emphasize those traits in your life.

A positive action to change a negative ancestral pattern
doesn't need to be immense or earth-shattering. It can be a
small act, as long as it is going in the right direction. For
example, if there are workaholics on both sides of your family
and you are a workaholic, a small action might be making
a commitment to do nothing for an hour every Sunday. Or
perhaps you might decide to take half an hour every day to
read a novel. When you make a pact with yourself to take
action, make only commitments that you can keep. It is
better to reserve one minute a day for relaxation, and then
to keep your commitment, than to commit to an hour and
not follow through. *Do not give your word lightly. And when*
you do give your word, keep it. Whether you give your word to
yourself or to another, it is the same thing. Ultimately, your com-

mitment is always to yourself. There are times in life when, for one reason or another, it is hard to keep your word. Rather than either feeling guilty or blithely ignoring the fact that you haven't been true to your word, make amends to yourself and anyone else involved, and then forgive yourself and get on with life.

Evaluation Exercise 2

The way we relate to friends and family can often be traced back to our ancestral roots. Listed below are descriptions of qualities that relate to relationships:

accepting, loving, judgmental, fearful, closed-off, expressive, compassionate, sad, angry, stoic, withdrawn, domineering, dutiful, passionate, frustrated, callous, violent, abusive, acquiescent, withdrawn, sweet, loyal, kind, bored, honest, dishonest, stagnant, dynamic, spiritual, conservative, reticent

1. Find the words that best describe what *you perceive* your ancestors' attitudes to their relationships to be. Write the qualities on your chart.

2. Which of the words describe your attitude to your relationships? Note if there is a similarity between your list of qualities and your ancestral list of qualities.

3. If there are positive qualities that you share with your ancestors, it is valuable to acknowledge and honor the ancestors who may have helped contribute to those attributes.

4. If there are negative attributes that you share with your generational family, look to see what action you can take to begin to de-emphasize those traits in your life.

Evaluation Exercise 3

A very powerful way that family and ancestral patterns influence us is through the sexual rules and sexuality patterns that are passed down. For example, research has shown that parents who abuse their children were usually abused as children. Although the nature of sexual expression passed down through the ancestors is very likely not something that your relatives may want to discuss, it is valuable to pursue this investigation for your own self-understanding. There is strong evidence to support the theory that the sexual behavior of one generation dramatically influences the behavior and the attitudes of the next. Do you perceive that the members of your family and your ancestors in regards to sexuality were:

free and open, conservative, violent, abusive, tender, loving, salacious, lusty, bawdy, perverse, frigid, angry, afraid, faithful, unfaithful, loyal, dutiful, disgusted, controlling, carefree, joyous, apathetic, sensual, disinterested, overly interested

1. Find the words that best describe what *you perceive* your ancestors' attitudes to their sexuality to be. Write the qualities down.

2. Which of the words describe your attitude to sex? Note if there is a similarity between your list of qualities and your ancestral list of qualities.

3. If there are positive qualities that you share with your ancestors, it is valuable to acknowledge and honor the ancestors who may have helped contribute to those attributes.

4. If there are negative attributes that you share with your

generational family, look to see what action you can take to begin to de-emphasize those traits in your life.

Evaluation Exercises can also be done in additional areas, such as money, health, religion, initiative and drive, creativity, food, and education—or in any other area of interest or significance to you. The more knowledge and awareness you gain about the emotional legacy passed down to you by your ancestors, the easier it is to heal it.

4. Creating New Family Patterns

You will always have a past; the ancestral soul dwells inside you. But as you evaluate the influence of your family on your life, you are ready to begin to heal the past and create new, more loving family patterns for the future.

Exercise: Cutting the Cords
of Ancestral Negativity

The following is a guided meditation to help you love your family and ancestors for who they are, not necessarily for their deeds.

You are on top of a hill. One by one your ancestors walk up the winding path to the top of the hill. You are holding the staff of truth, and when each one approaches, you can see into his or her heart and soul. The staff that you hold gives

---

you great compassion and understanding. You can see the challenges and the triumphs that each individual has encountered in life. With infinite compassion, imagine saying to them, "I accept you for who you are." As each ancestor stands before you, notice the space between the two of you. We often have unseen but very real psychic connections between ourselves and others. If you notice any negative lines of energy flowing between the two of you, you are free to imagine yourself cutting the cords that connect you to this individual. This doesn't necessarily mean that you are cutting the connection with this ancestor; it means that you are severing any negative psychic influence this person may have over you. As you say good-bye to your ancestors and watch them walk away, send them your blessings. Know that the blessings your ancestors receive from you will circle their way through time back to you.

CREATING A NEW IDENTITY

One of the difficulties in creating new family patterns lies in forming a new identity. Often your identity is so interwoven with your family's that when you begin to break out of it, there might be a period of time when you don't know who you are. This can be very disorienting and even discouraging. For example, Sam did a substantial amount of inner work to break free of negative family patterns. He came from a very close-knit family that had an extraordinary distrust of strangers. He wanted to break free of that ancestral pattern, to become more open and loving in all his relationships. However, as he began to break free of this family trait, *he* began to feel like a stranger in his family. This experience shook him to his core, and there was a time when he became unsure of who he was. His own definition of himself was so closely connected with the definition that his family had of him that when his old identity began to change, he was very confused and uncertain. He decided that his best course of action was to spend time away from his family in order to develop his new sense of self. Eventually, he was able to reunite with his family in a strong and positive way. He told me that he noticed his family members had become more accepting as a result of his openness. A period of adjustment, although uncomfortable, is nevertheless important as one begins to discover a new sense of self.

Sometimes, when you begin to release a negative family pattern, you may feel out of place in your family. As you free yourself from old negative patterns, the people who love you the most may often be the most resistant to the changes you are going through. Of course, this doesn't always happen. Sometimes families are very supportive of change. Jacki had a severe spider phobia. It was so severe that she couldn't eat a tomato if the stem was on it because it looked like a spider. Her mother, as well as her grandparents and great-grandmother, had the same phobia. When she released this ancestral pattern, her family celebrated her success rather than regale her with justifications about why people should be afraid of spiders. Every time you change or release a negative family pattern,

*Exercise: Assessment
of Relationships with Your
Living Family*

To evaluate realistically your relationship with
each of your living family members ask yourself
these questions:

- How do I feel after I have been with this person?
  Drained? Supported? Energized? Depressed? Just
  okay?
- What am I getting from this relationship?
- What is this family member getting
  from me?
- Do I participate in destructive behavior when I
  am with this individual or afterward?
- Does this person empower and support me or
  insult and criticize me?
- Does the value I gain from being with this
  individual outweigh the negative aspects of this
  relationship?
- How will this person react if I change or release
  an old family pattern?

*Exercise: Assessment
of Relationships with
Your Ancestors*

Even though your ancestors are dead, you are still
in relationships with them. In creating a new
identity and new family patterns, it is also
important to evaluate your relationships with your
ancestors.

Go through each ancestor (see chapter 2 for
definition of your ancestors) and ask these
questions:

- How do I feel about this individual?
- Do I gain value from this relationship?
- Do I feel that I would have been judged by this
  individual?
- Are there expectations this individual would
  have had of me?
- Would I have been disappointing to this person?
- What form do I want my relationship
  to take?
- How would this person have reacted to my
  changing an ancestral pattern?

you create a new identity. This new sense of self can change the dynamics of your current relationships; for this reason, you might want to spend time analyzing the dynamics of your relationships with your living family as well as your ancestral family before making a major change. There are some exercises on pages 92–93 to help you with this family assessment.

After you have assessed your relationships, you may need to make some choices. Honoring your roots and your familial ties doesn't necessarily mean that you need to spend time or energy with your family. Sometimes the healthiest way to honor your roots is to spend time away from your family. Then you can decide if you want to be with them in a new way, or perhaps not be with them at all.

ASKING YOUR ANCESTORS TO HELP YOU CREATE
NEW FAMILY PATTERNS

Visualization exercises are an excellent way to access the subconscious mind. In the same way that dreams offer messages from the subconscious mind, creative visualizations can give you valuable information about yourself and your past that might not be readily available to your conscious mind. Numerous traditions around the world employ the use of an Ancestral Teacher. In those cultures, individuals will often call on the ancestral teacher, who is a being that embodies all the wonderful qualities of all the collective ancestors. An exercise you can use to ask your Ancestral Teacher how you can create new family patterns follows.

*Exercise: Ancestral
Teacher*

Imagine yourself walking in a beautiful place in nature. In this sanctuary of nature, you become more at peace with yourself with every step you take. Ahead of you is a large orb of white shimmering light. Step into this luminous light. Become aware of this light enveloping you with protection and blessings. Take a moment to experience being filled with light. Step out of the light sphere and find yourself drawn to a still pool. This is the Pool of Ancestral Truth. On the other side of this pool is your Ancestral Teacher. As you kneel next to this pool, you can see images of past times reflected gently on the pool's surface. As you ask questions of the teacher, the images on the pool change, showing you valuable information about the past that can be used for healing the family tree.

Some questions that you may ask are:

- What are the most valuable traits that I have gained from my predecessors?
- How may I best use these qualities within myself to be of value to the universe?
- What are the negative tendencies within me that have been transmitted from the past?

- What is the best way for me to heal the cycle?

You can then thank your Ancestral Teacher and return to waking consciousness.

CHANGING YOUR POINT OF VIEW OF THE PAST

Your relationship to the past is based on your memories, both conscious and subconscious. These memories generate your behavior because your present behavior is based on your past behavior. Your memories are also affected by your present point of view. By changing your point of view, you can alter the context in which you view your memories; this, in turn, allows you to create new familial patterns. For example, if you have the point of view that all your past experiences were valuable lessons, then all your memories will be imbued with important lessons. If your point of view is that your past was completely miserable, then your memories will coincide with this. All history, whether oral or written, has been construed to align with an ideology or a point of view. As unlikely as it sounds, you can change the structure or context in which you hold your past by changing your point of view. When you change your point of view, you can change your present and even your probable future and can help create new family patterns. The exercise that follows can help you shift your point of view by restructuring the past.

Restructuring the Past

The exercise below is one of the most powerful exercises I have experienced. I use it in my seminars with remarkable results. It allows you to journey back in time to view yourself as a child and then further back in time to view and have an impact on your parents and grandparents as children. I believe the strength of this exercise lies in the malleable nature of the past. We are educated to believe that the past is staid and unmovable. However, I believe that the past can change, which then affects the present and the future.

Even if you don't believe that it is possible actually to change the past, remember that the past dwells in your DNA and in the memory cells of your brain. Change the past that dwells inside your brain, and you change the subsequent negative patterns attached to that past. This exercise can help you change age-old patterns that have culminated and been passed down from those memories. It can be done whether your parents and grandparents are living or have passed on.

To program yourself for this inward journey, ask someone to read the following to you in a very soothing voice. You can also tape-record yourself reading the exercise to play back at a later time. (If you are making a tape, substitute "I" for "you" in the process.) It is such an important exercise that I have included it in its entirety on page 98–102.

You can heal the past. It can be done lovingly and gently, yet firmly. Hold a vision of what you want to accomplish. Keep your focus on that goal. Remember that everything that has happened to you has allowed you to grow spiritually. There is value in your past, no matter what form it has taken. Perhaps it has made you more compassionate toward the suffering of others. Perhaps it has allowed you to become a

*Exercise: The Journey to
Your Immediate Ancestors*

Begin by getting your body into a very relaxed
position, either sitting or reclining. Start by taking
some very deep, relaxed breaths. With each breath
you take, you are becoming more and more
relaxed. Each breath you take, each sound you
hear, allows you to become more and more relaxed.
[Allow a period of silence here.]

Good. Now place your awareness on your left
foot and allow it to relax. It is now very relaxed.
Now put your attention on your right foot and feel
it let go and relax. Imagine a wonderful feeling of
relaxation rolling up both your legs the way that
waves roll up to the shore. Good. Continue to
imagine warm, slow waves of relaxation rolling up
from your feet, through your legs, up your torso, out
of your arms, and up and out of the top of your
head. Your entire body is now relaxed and warm
and comfortable as wave after wave of relaxation
rolls through your body. Take one very deep breath
and totally relax and let go.

Begin by going back in time in your own life.
Imagine an event from earlier today. Make it seem
as real as you can. Really place yourself back into
that memory. Remember the smells, colors, and
sounds. Recall what people were saying and what

you were feeling, both physically and emotionally. Recall as much detail as you can. Now let that memory go.

Go back to a memory from yesterday. Completely immerse yourself in that memory. Now let it go. Go back to a memory approximately one week ago. Don't be concerned if a memory pops into your mind that isn't from exactly one week ago. Whatever memory appears is the right one. Recall it as thoroughly as possible, and then release it. Continue going backward in time through your memories. Each time, after immersing yourself in the memory, let it go. [Repeat the following slowly and carefully, allowing time for a memory to surface before releasing it. This part of the exercise is helpful because it allows patterns to surface that can be released later during the exercise.]

Now go to a memory when you were happy. Let it go.
Go to a memory when you were sad. Let it go.
Go to a memory when you were angry. Let it go.
Go to a memory when you were peaceful. Let it go.
Go to a memory when you were grieving. Let it go.
Go to a memory when you were silly. Let it go.
Go to a memory when you were excited. Let it go.
Go to a memory when you were afraid. Let it go.
Go to a memory when you were in love. Let it go.
Go to a memory when you were resentful. Let it go.

Go to a memory when you were feeling wise. Let
it go.

Now go to a memory when you were
approximately eighteen years old. Let it go. Go
back to age sixteen. Continue traveling back in
time, backward through your childhood: age fifteen
. . . fourteen . . . thirteen . . . twelve . . . eleven . . .
ten . . . nine . . . eight . . . seven . . .
six . . . five . . . four . . . three . . . two . . . one . . . six
months . . . three months . . . one month . . .

You are continuing your journey back in time,
traveling back in time, beyond your present life,
back into the womb . . . and beyond. You are now
traveling back to the time when your mother [or
the person that you identified as mother] was a
very small child. Really imagine this. See her as a
small child, perhaps in a time of need. No matter
what your relationship was like with her in later
life, right now she is a small, unhappy child. Take
this child, put her on your lap, and comfort her.
Hold her and rock her. Let her know she is cared
for. You know the challenges and difficulties ahead
for her, and you give her understanding and love.
Imagine a beautiful light surrounding both of you.
This light infuses a wonderful energy within her
spirit that will weave its way through her life and

through her to you. Now see her laughing and happy, running off into the sunshine.

[If you are making a tape, repeat the above part of this meditation regarding seeing your mother as a small child, but go back to the time when your father (or the person that you identified as father) was a small boy. You can repeat the above exercise with each of your maternal grandparents and your paternal grandparents. See each of these individuals as small children, each in a time of need. You can do this even if you don't remember your grandparents. Just imagine what they may have been like as small children. Then imagine infusing each individual with vibrant, healthy, loving energy as you did with your mother. This will help them throughout their lives. You are positively influencing the past, and this, in turn, has a positive effect on you and your future.]

Now . . . it is time, gently and easily, to return to your present life. Just allow all the images and memories to fade away, just drift away. As you slowly find yourself returning to normal consciousness, take a few moments to adjust yourself to present time.

Good.

As you move more and more toward normal waking awareness, you feel good, strong, and empowered. You have stepped into your far past with courage and have looked without judgment at who and what you have been. By this very looking, your present life is enhanced and enriched. By this very observing, you have taken a step closer to the divinity within you. You are free to explore any past time, and the knowledge you gain creates the space for your life to be more fulfilling and whole.

I'm going to count from one to five. When I reach five, you will be totally awake and aware. One . . . two: Your body is healthy and strong. Three: More and more awake. Four: Your eyes feel as if they have been bathed in fresh cool spring water. Five: Wide awake and feeling great. Open your eyes now. Stretch and enjoy the beauty of the day.

stronger human being. The roots of trees grow deepest where the wind blows the hardest. The Dalai Lama said that we do not learn tolerance from our friends (but from those who irritate us). Hold your past as a precious gift. Beneath the pain and suffering, there is value to be garnered from each of your experiences as well as from the emotional legacy you gained from your forebears. The spirit of appreciation and thankfulness for what you have been given will allow the future to unfold for you in beauty.

4

Empowering Your Descendants

I had the privilege of spending time in Africa with the most honorable Credo Vusamazulu Mutwa, the spiritual leader of the Zulu people. This remarkable man is a revered visionary and prophet to his people. He shared with me the wonderful way in which the ancient ones empowered their descendants.

Our ancestors were very, very aware of us. In fact, if you look back into history, you will find that our forebears did many things that they did not need to do, but they did them out of awareness of our presence. For example, they wrote things on stone walls and inscribed things in very hard stone, and then put these things in most inaccessible places to be found by their descendants. These engravings were put in dangerous and difficult-to-reach places. They wanted us to know that they were there, and they were giving us knowledge that we have not grasped, in our great stupidity.

Ancient people didn't build their temples simply for burial. This wasn't the main purpose; in fact, the bodies buried inside the temples were a way of protecting them. In England and Europe, important people are buried inside cathedrals. This does not mean that the cathedral is made for burying people . . . burying people in a cathedral gives the cathedral a certain charisma which discourages certain types of vandals. Ancient temples were created for the descendants.

Our ancestors and the people of the most remote past were very aware of us. They tried, in many ways, to warn us about the potential for cataclysms that could shake the world apart. There was no personal concern for themselves . . . the ancient people were trying to warn us. They knew that they would die centuries and centuries before the end of the world. However, they were so full of love for us that they wanted us to know that they were more concerned about us than they were about themselves. [Through their visions] they saw the floods of the future, they saw future earthquakes, they saw the deaths of hundreds of millions of animals, and they wanted to warn us of our own particular danger. Why? Because they were filled with an overwhelming love and pity for us. This is why I say that this book about ancestors and descendants is a very important book.

Our forefathers and our ancient mothers were full of love for us. They felt responsible for us, and just as they protected their immediate offspring, so they tried to protect their far, far offspring. They wanted us not to come to any harm, and for this reason, they tried to pass on knowledge in many forms, some of which we are not even able to grasp today. Do we even think about human beings of a thousand years from now? We don't. As a culture we are selfish, self-centered, and blind, but those ancient people were not blind. The men and the women who left us thousands of artefacts, thousands of mathematical calculations, and warned us in so many ways about what is to happen, were telling us that the cataclysms that are coming can be avoided. This is why, little one, I believe that the changes that are coming, which have been foreseen by ancient people, should not be called the end of the world but rather the rebirth of the human race.

Your actions and thoughts and love can empower and assist your descendants. Who are your descendants? How can you help them? This chapter gives you information on how to answer these questions and shows you how to have a positive impact on the coming seven generations.

TRACKING YOUR BIOLOGICAL DESCENDANTS

Your biological descendants are obvious. If you have children and grandchildren, these are your blood descendants. They may look like you. They may share your hair color, eye color, or temperament. There is a powerful connection between you and your blood descendants. They carry genetic encoding from your DNA, just as you carry encoding from your ancestors.

One of the most powerful spiritual experiences I have had was going into a deep meditation and actually tracking my descendants. I was particularly drawn to my great-grandson. I saw him at age seven. He was small for his age. His eyes were bright; his spirit was shining. He had a strong sixth sense and a deep connection to nature. Although he wasn't consciously aware of me, I knew he could feel the love that I was pouring into him. I knew he was open to spiritual realms.

You can track your blood descendants through time and even glimpse into their lives. You can do this through meditation and visualization. Meditation is not necessarily just an exercise for your imagination. You can actually visit your descendants. There are portals into the future through which anyone can travel to observe and even to offer assistance. This is not a unique ability, evidenced by the many documented cases of clairvoyance. Since the beginning of civilization, people have received accurate information regarding the future. Many ancient predictions have been fulfilled, dreams have correctly foretold the future, and ordinary people have received clear premonitions. Questions about how this can occur have fascinated both philosophers and scientists.

To understand how you can observe and make a difference to your descendants through meditation, it is necessary to examine the nature of time. In normal life, the space around us is measured by height, length, and breadth. However, scientist Albert Einstein declared that space and time are inseparable and together they are what he called a space-time continuum. He showed that both time and space are elastic and that they both expand and contract and, in fact, can warp themselves into four-dimensional curves. Hence, time can loop back upon itself. Though this sounds confusing, in the realm of sophisticated mathematics, it is completely logical. And to those who live in native cultures, the cyclical nature of time is as natural as the air they breathe.

Exercise: Journey to Meet
Your Biological Descendants

Imagine that you are on a beach on a hazy summer morning. The waves of the sea are gently ebbing and flowing over golden sand. The air is fresh and clean. As you walk along the shore, you can see in the distance a large ten-foot shimmering sphere resting lightly on the sand. Its surface seems to be an opalescent silver that reflects a soft muted light from the sun. As you approach the sphere, you can hear a subtle hum or vibration emanating from it, which intensifies as you get nearer.

Abruptly, the hum ceases, and a door opens into the sphere. You step inside, and find yourself sitting on a comfortable chair. Although no one can see into the sphere, you can see out very clearly. The door closes. Very lightly, the sphere rises up from the shore. You watch as the sphere travels higher and higher. As you look down, you can see the planet covered with swirling mists. These are the mists of time. You know that beneath the dense cover of the mists, time is changing. The planet is going forward in time.

Gently and easily, your sphere begins to descend, until you land in an area near one of your biological descendants. When you arrive, you are free to leave the sphere and explore the world of your descendant. You can travel farther and farther forward in time in your time sphere, each time landing near one of your descendants. Whenever you encounter your heirs, you are free to communicate with them and give them advice and guidance based on what you have learned in your life.

When you have finished, you can return to the present time in the sphere, knowing that you have made a positive and loving impact on your descendants.

A meditation where you travel into the future can be likened to a time overlap, or a fold in time, where you have a window into the future. Scientists call these windows in time *cosmic wormholes*, from the idea that a worm can take a shortcut by boring a hole through an apple rather than going around it. Even if you are not actually traveling to the future, the act of imagining the journey can begin to help change the collective unconscious for the whole planet. The more people who believe in the reality of the next seven generations and beyond, the more of a chance our descendants have.

You can use this exercise again and again, each time deepening your relationship with your future kin. You may meet the same individuals each time you journey, or you may meet the ever-broadening span of your blood descendants.

SPIRITUAL DESCENDANTS

Your impact on your spiritual descendants is no less viable than your impact on your biological descendants. Your spiritual descendants are the children and grandchildren and so on of those whom you have influenced in your life, even if they were not related to you. In addition, in our modern world, many people are part of split families. A child that you raise, whether adopted or a stepchild, is nevertheless your descendant. You affect his or her life and destiny no less powerfully than you do those of someone who shares your genes. Even if you have no children, you still have spiritual descendants. People without children deeply affect our world. Some of the people who have left the most indelible mark on history were childless.

Your realm of influence reaches far beyond the boundaries of your immediate life. It reaches the many people that you have had interactions with throughout your life, and it reaches the children of those people. You may never know the impact you have, but you do change the world through your actions and experiences. Perhaps the day that you let a woman go in front of you at the grocery store because she seemed in a hurry started a positive chain reaction. Maybe the woman was contemplating whether to let her daughter go to the college of her daughter's choice or to the one that she went to. Your momentary generosity paved the way for the mother to decide to allow her daughter to go to the college of her choice. The mother's decision meant that the child discovered a vaccine for a dangerous virus because that university had a better laboratory than her mother's college. Your actions can and do affect the future progeny of the world. To track and empower your spiritual descendants, here is an exercise you can do.

---

*Exercise: Journey to Meet
Your Spiritual Descendants*

Imagine a beautiful meadow in a clearing
surrounded by a circle of thick mist. The meadow is
filled with bright golden sunshine, lush green grass,
a sprinkling of spring flowers, and the morning
songs of birds. In the center of the meadow is a
large round table. This is the table where your
spiritual descendants will gather. Imagine sitting at
the table. There is a chair that has been especially
designated for you. One by one, out of the
surrounding mists, step some of your spiritual
descendants. Each one takes a place at the table.
Magical goblets filled with healing springwater
appear at each setting. As you lift your goblet to
toast the future, your descendants add their toasts
to yours. This is the gathering time. You can ask
questions of each individual descendant, or you can
discuss as a group any topic you wish. As a group,
you can also send energy and healing to any place
or any time (past, present, or future) in the world.

You can use this exercise again and again, each time deepening your relationship with your future kin. You may meet
the same individuals each time you journey, or you may
meet the ever-broadening span of your spiritual descendants.

GIFTS TO THE FUTURE

There are many different ways to send gifts to your descendants. The most important aspect to this activity is that you are consciously sending love and faith and hope to those who will follow you. By caring enough about your descendants to send them gifts, you are helping to ensure their time on earth will be better. They will be able to feel the loving energy and the faith you had for them in the gifts that they receive. These qualities will be present in whatever gifts you send and may kindle love and hope and happiness in their lives.

Life-History Letter

A wonderful gift you can give to your descendants can be in the form of a letter to your seventh-generation descendants. Write about your life history. This letter can be a warm and intimate account, telling your descendants what was most important to you in your life. You can tell them about the experiences that shaped your life, the lessons that taught you what you most needed to learn, and the information you most want to pass on to them.

Include specific details about what your life was like. Not only will this be fascinating for them to read at some far point in the future, but also you never know what information will be particularly relevant and useful to them. Perhaps they will be facing similar difficulties in their lives; the particulars of their problems may be different, but perhaps some small discovery that you made could save them pain and trouble.

Tell your descendants about the people you love, the places and books and animals that touched your life in a vital way. Share your dreams for the future, for their lives. This is a very direct and personal way to share the love you have and want to send to them. They will actually be reading your words years and years from when you wrote them.

You might want to share this letter with your children. They might want to add letters of their own to travel along with yours through time to your mutual descendants. If you are childless, you will want to decide to whom you desire to give your letter. Find someone younger than you whom you trust and love. Perhaps a niece or nephew, or someone with whom you have worked closely for years. Explain that you want to pass on information about what your life was like and that you want to share this tradition with them. It is a sacred trust that not everyone will feel able to undertake. It is a real responsibility, so do not resent it if someone you care for does not believe that he or she can take this on. Just know that someone else who does want to do this will come along when the time is right.

"If I Had My Life to Live Over Again" Letter

Another type of letter you can write to your descendants is one that delineates what you would do differently if you could live your life over again. You can also write this from the viewpoint that you are at the end of your life, reviewing your life and realizing what you might like to change. This can be a powerful exercise for you, as well as a way to provide valuable insight for your descendants.

Here is part of the letter that I wrote to my descendants. As I wrote it, I felt an immense love and dedication for each of them. I knew I would continue to support and love each one long after my body was gone.

Dear Descendants,

If I had my life to live over again, I would like to take more time to listen to others rather than spending time defending my point of view. I would be sillier and more willing to make a fool of myself. I wouldn't take life so seriously, and I would laugh a lot more, especially at myself. I would push myself to take more risks. I would love my body no matter what shape it was in, and I wouldn't apologize for things that had nothing to do with me.

I would love deeply and fully without fear of rejection. I would be kind to people for no reason, without ever expecting anything in return. I would forgive myself instantly rather than carry guilt and recrimination. I wouldn't be in such a hurry; I would relax more, have more fun, spend more time with friends, dance in the rain, and sing out loud to my heart's content, even if I couldn't carry a tune.

Perhaps, dear descendants, these are things that you learn only after living life, but if my experiences can help you in the smallest way, it will make the struggles that I have gone through so much easier to bear. I believe in you. I have seen you in my dreams and my visions. You have my love. I will continue to send you my love through time and space.

Your Ancestor,
Denise

What Have You Learned in Your Life?

Another way to contribute to your descendants is to write down the wisdom that you have gained from your life experiences so it can be handed down to them. This not only benefits your descendants, but it can help you clarify for yourself what you have learned from your life lessons. Write it out and make copies. Keep one for yourself, and pass the other ones on to your biological and spiritual progeny. This list can accompany the life-history letter you pass down.

If I could gather all my descendants together when they are young and impressionable to give them wisdom based on my experiences and what I have learned over my lifetime, here is what I would want them to know.

GENERAL ADVICE

• Laugh as much and as often as you can. See the humor in life. Laugh at yourself, even in the difficult times. There was a time in my life when I was dying, or at least that was what the doctor told me. It was very serious. The plastic tube replacing my aorta had begun to separate from the vessel wall it was attached to. David, my husband, came into the room to see me. He looked so worried. Perhaps the melodrama of my impending death hit us both at the same time, because we began to laugh. For a few moments, our laughter escalated until peals of laughter bounded off the walls. I felt so good afterward. I don't know exactly what ignited our laughter, but I've always wondered if our laughter didn't contribute to the remarkable healing that occurred afterward.

• Never stop learning. No matter how old you are,

continue to learn. Learn new skills. Practice new talents. Learn a foreign language. I regret that I didn't learn a foreign language as a child. Learn to play a musical instrument. Learn first aid. It may save someone's life.

• Have a garden or at least cultivate some plants inside your home. Spend time in nature. Remember that all life is sacred.

INTEGRITY

• Live your life with integrity. Children usually have a strong sense of what is right and wrong. They know it is absolutely wrong to lie, cheat, or steal. When people get older, they are tempted to think in relative terms, e.g., "Everyone cheats on their taxes," "It's a big company. They can afford it if they accidentally overpaid me," "No one is going to care if I take a few pens from work." This is wrong. Maintain your integrity, even if you are the only one who knows. Never lie, cheat, or steal. However, there are times when there is higher integrity in following the dictates of the heart rather than in following an absolute. For example, sometimes lying is both necessary and even good, e.g., if you were hiding Jews in Nazi Germany. Listen to your heart and integrity will follow.

• Keep your word. Don't say it unless you mean it. Your word is your power. When you make a commitment to keeping your word, the universe will conspire to support you in that commitment.

QUIET THE MIND

• Be still and answers will come. Learn how to be silent, quiet your mind to watch for signs, and absorb wisdom from the universe. The world around you is always communicating to you.

• Slow down. Eliminate the superfluous from your life. Spend time alone. Simply be.

• At least once in your life, go on a Vision Quest. You are not on the planet just to survive. You are here for a purpose. Take time to retreat into nature in silence to discover your destiny and remember who you are.

THERE ARE NO ACCIDENTS

• Nothing is ever by chance. Whether or not you are conscious of it, the universe is unfolding exactly as it should for you. Your life will work when you choose to be where you are in your life.

• Where intention goes, energy flows. Whatever you put your attention on will expand. If you focus on that which is bright and beautiful, your life will be filled with beauty. If you focus on what's wrong with the world, you will be surrounded by a world in woe.

• Admit mistakes. Don't beat yourself up. Make amends and get on with life. Take responsibility for your life and don't blame others.

• Who you are is enough. If you don't think that you are all right the way you are, it takes an enormous amount of energy to change. When you accept that you are perfect exactly as you are, you will get better naturally. True peace comes by simply accepting others and yourself unconditionally, without expectations or demands. The moment you accept yourself completely as you are, life becomes wondrous and joyous. When you love who you are and what you are, nothing can touch you.

TAKING RISKS

• Life is a great and grand adventure. Jump in fearlessly and passionately, expecting the very best. Take risks. Don't shrink back from challenges. Embrace them. Rush toward them with passion and power. There are costs to taking risks, but they are far less than the long-range cost of comfort and inaction. If you are never embarrassed, scared, hurt, or insecure, it means that you have never taken any chances in life. Growth comes when you are willing to step beyond what is known and comfortable.

• Be bold. At the end of your life, you will probably regret the things you didn't do more than the things you did do. Will Rogers, a well-loved Cherokee orator, said, "Why not go out on a limb? That's where the fruit is." I couldn't say it better.

• Be unpredictable. Every once in a while be courageous. Embark on a madcap venture. When you are predictable, you begin to create ruts for yourself that become deeper with wear.

EMOTIONS

• No matter how old you are, be willing to allow your inner childlike nature to express itself. Have fun. Be spontaneous. Laugh when you are happy. Cry when you are sad. Be silly. Clap your hands with glee and joy. Giggle. Love deeply and fully.

• Time is an invention of the modern world. Only here and now is real. If you are harboring regrets from the past or worries about the future, you are not experiencing the magnificent potential available to you right now. When you draw your energy into the present time, then, remarkably, creativity, peace, and power explode within you.

• To release fear, make a decision, even if that decision is to feel afraid. Whenever you find you cannot conquer fear, then choose your fear, choose to be afraid. When you consciously become the source of your own fear, you are in control, and consequently, fear loosens its hold on you.

HANDLING LIFE'S DIFFICULTIES

• Whenever you are faced with a difficulty, imagine the very worst that could happen. When you can accept that possibility, then you can handle whatever life brings you.

• Life always goes in circles, and every part of the great circle of life is sacred. Your life will have times that are fallow. These are essential for the time of harvest.

• You do not have to suffer to grow. We are born into a collective unconscious that states that suffering builds character. You can, in fact, grow spiritually in leaps and bounds without ever suffering. Whenever the allure of suffering attracts you, say to yourself, "I do not need to suffer to grow."

• The past is malleable. If you want to change your present circumstances, change the past that exists in your mind.

• You will outgrow situations, places, and even some people. Be willing to let go. When one door in your life closes, another will open.

• Don't waste time wishing you were someone else or somewhere else. You are where the party is. Accept and affirm that where you are is the most exciting place to be, and the universe will come tumbling to you.

• Your life is guided. The suffering that appears in your life has a purpose. Look for its lesson.

CAREER

• If your work isn't challenging, inspiring, or absorbing, don't do it. What ignites your enthusiasm, optimism, and zest for life? When you discover that, you will know what your true life's work is.

• Make decisions based on joy rather than what's practical or logical. Follow your heart. Follow your dreams.

• Flowers open when they are ready. God doesn't force them open. There is a clear pattern flowing through your life; don't try to force things. Everything has its own time.

• Whatever you do, do it well.

• I have learned much more from my failures than my successes. Do not be afraid of failing. We often discover what will work by finding out what won't work. It takes courage to take risks in your career, but the individual who never makes mistakes never really succeeds.

• Stay out of debt. Make it a priority. Pay bills on time. Pay your bills before spending money on anything else except absolute necessities.

• When setting out on your own, don't worry if you don't have enough money. Sometimes limited finances can be a blessing in disguise, allowing you to activate your creativity and opening you to opportunities that you wouldn't be aware of if you were completely financially secure.

RELATIONSHIPS

• Take time to enjoy your family and friends. I am convinced that the key to life is relationships. Nothing—not power, money, or fame—can substitute for your friends and family, and nothing can bring them back once they are gone.

• Everyone and everything around you is your teacher.

• Spend time learning to understand others' points of view. Know that if you had the same upbringing and genetic encoding, you would act exactly as they act. Let go of always having to be "right." Don't obstinately hold on to your opinions. All opinions are viewpoints, and all viewpoints are limited. Learning this can make an enormous difference in your life.

• Love is the unconditional acceptance of another being. This doesn't necessarily mean that you love people's actions, but that you love who they are as deeply and fully as you can.

• Don't be afraid to say "I don't know," "I need help," "You are right," "I made a mistake," "I'm sorry."

• Everyone and everything is your mirror. You do not see things as they are. You see things as *you* are.

• If you are my male descendant, cherish the females in your life. Learn about the opposite sex, and understand that they are different from men. That understanding will make your life a lot easier.

If you are my female descendant, cherish the males in your life. Learn about the opposite sex, and understand that they are different from women. That understanding will make your life a lot easier.

• You can truly give only as much as you are willing to receive.

• Never diminish anyone's hope. Empower the dreams and visions of others, and you will be empowered. Celebrate the success of others, and you will succeed.

• Don't use profanity. Every word you speak has an energy associated with it, and every word will either lower or raise your energy. Whenever we communicate, there is an exchange of energy. Profanity lowers your energy and lowers the energy of the person you are speaking to. When you know the power of your words, you become more careful with your communications.

• Meticulously return all that you borrow, and never lend anything unless you are willing to let it go if it doesn't return to you.

• Learn to find enjoyment wherever you are and with whoever you are with.

YOUR HOME

• Your home is a metaphor for your life. Create beauty and peace around you, and your life will be more peaceful.

• If there are things in your home that you don't love or use, get rid of them. They clog your energy. When you clear the clutter out of your home, hold the intention that you are clearing out the cobwebs in your soul and it will be so. The universe responds to symbolic acts.

• Create a place in your house that is sacred. Make a home altar or a shrine, and place objects on it that are spiritually meaningful to you. Your altar then becomes a center point for inviting the divine into your home.

- Bring nature into your home. We have become separated from our connection to the earth. To reignite this connection, place objects from the natural world in your home.
- If you want more peace in your life, create a peaceful environment. If you want more prosperity in your life, create an environment that feels abundant. By using your home as a metaphor, you create a constant subliminal message that helps propel you toward your destiny.

YOUR CHILDREN

- Encourage your children, and let them know how remarkable and unique they are.
- Do whatever you can to help your children have a good education.
- *Never* promise children anything that you know you cannot fulfill. Let them know through your actions that you are a noble being. They, in turn, will become noble beings.
- Listen to your children. Acknowledge their communications as valuable and worthwhile, and compassionately and lovingly keep them.

MIRACLES

- Believe in angels, magic, and miracles. They are real. Your life is guided. You are always surrounded by messengers from spirit, and they are only a thought away.
- You are a child of God. You have a right to be here. Your presence is a miracle.

If I Had One Month to Live
Letter

As an exercise, both for yourself and to pass down to your descendants, take time to imagine you have only one month to live. What would you do? An exercise such as this tends to make it crystal clear whether you are currently living the life that you desire. If your life is dramatically different from your answers, perhaps it's time to make some changes. Here are some peoples' answers.

If I had one month to live, I would:

- live each moment as fully as I could
- clean my house from top to bottom and organize all my papers before I did anything else
- videotape myself and leave it for my children
- tell my family and friends how much I love them
- go through my life to attempt to forgive or resolve all my relationships
- have a huge party, invite everyone I love, and ceremoniously give away everything I own
- spend time with my children and people I care about

- write about my life
- pray and meditate and spend time in nature talking to God
- go on a fabulous vacation somewhere warm and sunny

Planting a Generational Tree

I thank you for the seeds. . . . I'm too old to plant trees for my own gratification, I shall do it for my posterity.

—FROM A LETTER WRITTEN BY THOMAS JEFFERSON, 1800

A traditional way of sending gifts into the future is by planting trees. When you walk through an ancient forest, you can feel the grandeur, the wisdom, and the stability of these noble beings. Feelings of awe are often evoked when we stop to consider just how long these trees have been on the earth. They give so much in terms of beauty, shade, food, and improved air quality. Their roots go down deep into the body of the earth, anchoring the soil and preventing erosion. Their leaves and branches provide homes for many birds and animals.

When you plant a tree, you are enhancing the quality of life of people and creatures whom you may never meet, but you can have the knowledge that this is a gift that will go on giving long after you are gone. Plant trees all your life. That way you know that you have helped to make the world a better and more beautiful place. Trees gladden the lives of everyone, and they are essential to the health of our planet. They are an important legacy. When planting trees, you may want to plant a special tree specifically dedicated to your future progeny. Planting a generational tree is an act of hope and faith; it is a sacred act. The trees that you plant for your descendants will continue to radiate those feelings to them and into the world for as long as they live.

Carefully choose the spot where you plant your generational tree. Have you ever entered a beautiful, old garden where, even though the paths and plants have become overgrown, you can still feel all the love and artistry that went into the making of the garden originally? These gardens have a secret and magical feel to them because of the intention and care of the people who planted them. Think carefully about how your generational tree will grow, how its shade will fall, how it will best look from several different vantage points. Find out how large it will be when mature, and then be sure to leave it plenty of room to grow.

There is power in beginnings, so once you have decided the best location for your generational tree, you might want to have a dedication ceremony for the planting. During your ceremony, clearly state your intention for the tree and for your descendants. If you plant a generational tree with deliberate focus and ceremony, the earth and the seedling will be imbued with an energy field that will continue to emanate from the tree for years to come.

It is a nice idea to plant a tree where your descendants may always be able to see it, for instance, on a piece of land in the country. But even if that is not possible, whenever you plant a tree, you are making a symbolic act that leaves a positive heritage. With the constant mobility and fast pace of modern life, it is a real possibility that a tree you plant might be cut down at some point in time. Or perhaps your family may move far away from where you planted it. Because of this, you may also want to adopt a tree as your generational tree. Find a tree in a park or a conservatory, or somewhere it is unlikely to be cut down, and adopt it as your generational tree. Let your children or your spiritual descendants know that this is their tree. Explain to them that the trees are our brethren, and tell them about the living spirit within each tree. You may even have them name their adopted tree as this helps form a deeper connection to it. You can plant many generational trees in your lifetime. You may want to record where they are planted and pass this information down to your descendants. Every tree, planted with love, leaves a legacy of hope for the future.

Blessing Ceremony for the
Generational Tree

Decide where the tree with be planted, taking into consideration soil conditions, sun, space for growth, and impact on the environment. Make sure that you have prepared the soil before your ceremony. Choose an auspicious day for the planting, such as an equinox or solstice or someone's birthday. Have an appointed time for the gathering for the tree-planting ceremony.

Stand in a circle around where the tree will be planted. The person who initiated the planting speaks about the purpose of the tree and makes a dedication such as:

> *I dedicate this tree to our descendants and to*
> *the future generations that follow. May you*
> *help contribute to a future that is filled with*
> *trees and flowers and joy for all living beings.*
> *May the Creator who dwells in all things fill*
> *you with love and light and peace. May you*
> *provide shade, beauty, and healing for all who*
> *come in contact with you.*

All those in the circle then place a handful of soil near the base of the tree, adding their blessings. To complete the dedication, have the youngest member of the gathering water the tree, saying:

> *May the waters of life nurture you, and*
> *may you grow in strength and harmony.*
> *You are loved.*

A tree planted in this fashion will radiate a much stronger life force throughout its entire life than a tree planted randomly or haphazardly.

Generational Box

Another kind of gift you can make to your descendants is a generational box. This is a more personal and private gift that you can create especially for the descendants in your family or for people whom you feel connected to as your spiritual descendants.

Deciding what to put into a generational box is a fun and very creative process. Before you actually choose what kind of a box you want, give some thought to what sorts of items you will be putting into it. The objects in the box will be a physical and symbolic collection of things that represent what was most important to you in your lifetime. They represent the legacy you want to leave to your descendants.

You might want to include family photos, a poem you loved over many years, or perhaps the feather that you found on the day you turned sixteen and realized what you wanted to do with your life. You should include some explanation of why you chose the items in your box. This will be of great interest to your descendants and will give them a sense of great personal connection to you. They will be able to hold in their hands the objects that you loved enough to put in the box that is now theirs. They will know that your hands touched those objects, your eyes read the words on those yellowed pieces of paper. And they will know that you cared enough about them to put this all together.

After you have decided what you want to put in the box, you can turn your attention to the box itself. There are numerous sorts of boxes that can last for many generations, such as boxes made of wood, pottery, or bamboo, antique boxes, new boxes, simple or ornate boxes. Pick a box that feels right to you. The box you choose is as symbolic as the objects you place within it.

You may want to discuss the box with your children or spiritual descendants. You can tell them its purpose, explaining that it is a gift that will be passed down by them to their children, who will, in turn, continue to pass it on. As you grow older, you might want to discuss who in your family is most interested in helping to keep the tradition going. Some children will probably feel a close connection with the process, while others might perceive it as a burden. You can be sure that there will always be family members who are interested in family history and who like to keep traditions alive. Those are the descendants who will want to be the keepers of the box. You can also make a number of boxes to hand down if more than one person wants to be the keeper of the box.

The process can be kept vital by each generation adding its own contributions to the box. Also, if more than one child or grandchild wants to carry on the tradition, the contents of the box can be divided and divided again, just as family photos and other mementoes are normally divided among various branches of a family.

Making the generational box is an important act of faith, and it is important to realize that the people who are supposed to take care of the box will step forward. It is not necessary to try and control the process once it has begun. The passing on of the box from one generation to the next can be a simple process. Some children will just naturally feel more of an affinity with the tradition than others. Neither response is better than the other, so there is no need for people to feel guilty because they do not have the time or stability or inclination to take care of the box.

Works of Art

Another wonderful way you can send gifts to your descendants is to create beautiful works of art and crafts to be handed down from one generation to the next. In older times, homes were never built with potential sale value in mind. Homes were built for one's children and grandchildren and their descendants. They were built for the generations. Similarly, household articles were made to last and to be passed on. Perhaps you or someone you know has a quilt that was made by a grand-mother or other forebear. Or perhaps your family has passed down beautiful pieces of handmade furniture. In families where there are excellent craftspeople, there is always pride in saying, "Oh, yes, my grandfather made that rocking chair!" You can re-create this kind of tradition in your own time, even if you haven't had it in the past. Pick a craft or art that you love best and make objects of beauty with the intention that they will be loved and kept by your descendants. All the care and creativity that you put into these things will shine out of them as beacons of your love for as long as they are passed on from one generation to the next.

Photographs and Videos

When misfortune occurs and a family is forced to flee from their home, the one item that most people regret losing is their family photos. Our photos (and videos) of our family and friends are a legacy that we can pass down to those beyond us. They allow us to feel part of a greater continuum of family. We can see physical similarities with family members whom we have never met. They connect us to our personal history. Going through family photos can offer valuable clues to our past. Who is included and who is excluded from a photo? How are the bodies positioned? Who is standing next to whom? What emotions and feelings seem to be present in the photo? In some cultures, it is believed that photos capture the soul. Perhaps in one respect this is accurate, because photos can reveal so much about individuals and their psyches at a given time in life.

Family photos can even help us to heal the past. For example, Caryn used a picture of herself as a child as a focal point to send love to her inner child. It helped her personal healing journey and allowed her to begin to repair the emotional damage done during her early childhood. Jack had a very difficult time with his father while growing up. As an adult, when his wife suggested putting up family pictures, his response was abruptly severe and negative. Jack realized that even looking at a photo of his father brought up uncomfortable emotions. His wife suggested that he find a photo of his father as a child and put it up. Over time, this had a remarkably healing effect on Jack. He was able to feel love for the child in the photograph, and that began to help melt the hatred he had for the adult the child grew up to be.

If you have a relative or ancestor with whom you have difficulty, find a photo of that individual, preferably at a young age, and really look at him or her. What do you see in the face? Is there pain or unhappiness beneath the countenance? Is there anything you wish to say to that person? As silly as it seems, speaking from your heart to the photo can have remarkable healing results.

Is there a relative or ancestor who you revere or who has qualities that you admire, perhaps a favorite aunt or great-grandparent? What are the qualities that you respect about this person? Putting the photo in a special place or a place of honor in your home or office is a positive way to assist you in developing these qualities more in your life. In this way, the photo acts as a subliminal reminder to inspire you to be the best you can be. In my office, I have a photo of my Cherokee grandmother overlooking my desk. I feel her compassion, integrity, and strength looking over my shoulder every day, and I am comforted.

Videos and photographs are wonderful ways of preserving the present for your descendants. Recording important family events, like holidays and weddings, will preserve what these rituals were like and will surely be valued by your descendants. However, also record ordinary conversations about everyday kinds of things. A film of your daughter's tea party with her toy bears or your husband hitting his thumb with the hammer when he is building a new room will be just as treasured as the wedding photos for the way they reveal what was most human about you.

Caring for Your Photo Legacy

- If you have any historic photos, make copies and distribute them to other family members, so if anything happens to one of them, there will still be others.
- Keep the negatives separate from the photos; even store them in a fireproof box.

- Make sure that your legacy photos have the date and name of each person in the shot. It can be discouraging to inherit "mystery photos."
- If you display your photos, make sure that they are out of the sun and are in acid-free mountings, so they will last over time. A professional framer can help you with the right materials.
- If you have children, make copies of the photographs and make an album for each child.
- Get acid-free scrapbooks and photo-safe albums to protect your photos. Over time, other sorts of albums can damage photos.

All these tangible gifts form a link, a living bridge between you and your descendants. They are tangible records of who you were, what you cared about, what made you the way you were. Wouldn't you love to know how your great-great-grandmother felt about the life she lived? How revealing it would be to know how your ancestors characterized themselves and their environment. Some people are lucky enough to have a few letters or parts of diaries from their forebears, and this helps them to understand themselves in view of the past. Let your descendants be able to count themselves this lucky, too.

Working for Causes You Believe In

In addition to the tangible gifts that we give to our progeny, there are powerful gifts of our actions and thoughts that we can contribute to their future well-being. One of the most powerful legacies you can leave for your descendants is to work for a cause that makes a contribution to the world (see chapter 6). As we approach the end of this millennium, many serious problems are confronting us. The problems are real, and they have the potential to threaten our very existence. But by choosing to take positive action rather than be paralyzed by fear or apathy, you can help create a brighter reality for your descendants. Walk your talk; no matter what action you take, whether it is small or large, it will help to make a difference to the future.

Cultural Inheritances

An important part of the legacy you will send to your descendants is the cultural inheritance that you pass on to them. You can enhance this legacy for them through the reinstatement of valuable traditions that have been a part of your heritage and by teaching these traditions to your children (see chapter 5). Perhaps your family has become alienated from the ethnic and cultural traditions of your ancestors. You can research these traditions and find authentic and meaningful ways to include them in your family's celebrations, holidays, and rituals. By doing this, you will be enriching the cultural inheritance that you leave for all those who come after you.

Retelling family stories, as well as folk tales and fables from your ethnic background, is a very powerful way of preserving the traditions of your family. Stories have been used from time immemorial as ways of preserving and passing on the values that were most important to groups of people. For example, your children and grandchildren will be fascinated to hear about how your grandmother survived the Great Depression and raised her eight children alone. This kind of story will help them to face difficulties they might encounter in their own lives. Telling the tales that have traditionally been told throughout the years in your culture will provide your children with a sense of their own history and will also provide them with a rich, cultural context for interpreting their lives.

Learning and passing on the traditional crafts and art forms of your cultural heritage is another important way of keeping these traditions alive for the generations who will follow you. Singing traditional songs, making traditional pots or rugs or clothing, will give your descendants a sense of pride in their heritage as well as a sense of connection and continuity with their ancestry. These objects and songs are tangible, audible ways of experiencing the past in the present. When you sing the same songs that your ancestors sang, when you prepare the traditional foods that they ate, you know in the most intimate way that you are all one. When you pass these skills, these objects, this knowledge, on to your children, who will, in turn, give them to their children, these priceless traditions continue to live and enhance the lives of each generation.

Clearing Yourself for Your Descendants

Perhaps the most powerful legacy you can leave for your progeny is clearing yourself of negative beliefs and emotional blockages (see chapter 3). When you conquer your inner demons, put lifelong addictions to rest, and remember who you are, you create an enormous energy that travels from you like a great tidal wave of light and love through the future. Clearing away your emotional wreckage will exponentially contribute to the future in ever-expanding circles. It is one of the finest and noblest gifts you can give the future.

5

Creating a
Spiritual Legacy

TRADITIONS, RITUALS, MYTHS, AND STORIES: CREATING THE SACRED AND PASSING IT ON

The psychological dangers through which earlier generations were guided by the symbols and spiritual exercises of their mythological and religious inheritance, we today . . . must face alone. This is our problem as modern, "enlightened" individuals, for whom all gods and devils have been rationalized out of existence.

—JOSEPH CAMPBELL, HERO WITH A THOUSAND FACES

The grand expanse of stars that once lit up the night sky has been dimmed into insignificance by the bright lights of our cities. The songs of the morning birds, which greeted our ancestors every day as they rose to tend their fields or go off on the hunt, have now been obliterated by the sounds of the morning commute. So, too, have the great rituals and myths become lost to us. Where once they marked and honored the vast mysteries of life and helped us to understand our transitions from one life phase to another, now they have become submerged in the swirling, fast pace of our busy and often disconnected lives.

There is an essential need within the human psyche to reinstate traditions, rituals, and myths in our lives. This need is evidenced by the increasing number of people asking "Who am I? What is my purpose?" The resurgence of fundamentalism and the popularity of the New Age movement as well as the advent of numerous spiritual associations attest to people's need to reinstate the holy, sacred, and mysterious into their lives.

One way to begin to fill the spiritual void in our culture is by reviving old traditions and creating new ones that can be passed on to our descendants. This is because traditions, rituals, and myths strengthen our connection to our past and our future as well as to the rhythms of nature and the universe. They are imbued with the substance of life and carry us to the essence of our being through re-establishing our divine communion with the cosmos. Joseph Campbell, the world's foremost authority on mythology, prior to his death in 1987, once wrote: "Myth is the secret opening through which the inexhaustive energies of the cosmos pour into human manifestations,"[1] and "It has always been the prime function of mythology and rite to supply the symbols that move the human spirit forward."[2]

Mythological stories and rites create meaning out of the complexities of the universe. They leave imprints on both our conscious and unconscious level that can serve as reference points throughout our lives. Mythology, ritual, and tradition serve as a kind of North Star to the traveler through life, bringing clarity and validation to the depth and texture of personal history as well as the history of whole eras and peoples. All the seemingly unconnected aspects of our lives are given significance and coherence through these systems for organizing separate, meaningless events into a rich structure that can give a sense of purpose to all experience.

As a child, I loved thunderstorms. I was forbidden from going outside during a storm because of the danger of being hit by lightning; however, often the excitement was too great, and I would do it anyway. Perhaps the tendency was generational, because my grandfather used to tie himself to a tree during the Oklahoma tornadoes so he could watch them.

It gave me great joy to dance wildly in the rain while thunder shook the earth. It made me feel vitally alive, as if I were made of the stuff of the wind and earth. I felt powerfully connected to all things, as I danced in the ecstatic ferocity with rain pounding my head and body. During my childhood, this was the closest that I came to experiencing the divine. Perhaps my storm dances emerged from the same wellspring from which myth and ritual came forth.

My friend Joseph Winterhawk Martin (Ariki Wairua) is a revered tohunga (spiritual leader) for the Taranaki Maori tribe in New Zealand. In a recent conversation, Joseph shared with me the importance that rituals and ceremonies have had in his life. His words deepened my understanding of the power of these ancient mysteries. He painted a beautiful picture of what it was like to grow up in a culture that revered the old ways and in which rituals and traditional stories still played a significant part in the training of the young.

In our tradition, we were taught at a young age to know and learn our history, about our family tree, and our songs, chants, legends, and stories. An old one would often call us together to sit under a tree and listen to the teachings. They taught us our spiritual way of life and how to communicate with our ancestors who had passed on. After each teaching, they showed us how to record what we had learned, so that we would remember every lesson.

Our old people were very strict in their teachings. We all had to learn the ceremonies and their importance in our way of life. We were also taught the ancient crafts and healing. We learned how to collect food and herbal medicines from the forest, rivers, lakes, streams, and the sea. We also learned the old traditions of storytelling. We gained knowledge of how to do things in a sacred way, and we were taught how to fast in order to receive a vision of the sacred things of our ancestors.

I can remember these days very clearly. There are not many left who can recall these teachings and sacred ways. Many of our people have gone the European way, leaving aside their Maori way of life. I miss those days with the old people, as so many of my teachers have now passed on.

RITUAL, TRADITION, AND CEREMONY

In ancient cultures, ceremonies were a part of life. Some ceremonies were long and took place over many days. Others were short, private rituals that were performed on a daily basis.

But every ceremony and ritual created deeper bonds to the participant's community and heritage.

Ceremonies marked the important moments that punctuated an individual's passage through life, such as the milestones of birth, entry into adulthood, and marriage. There were also ceremonies for healing, rituals to prepare warriors for battle and to welcome them home. These traditions emphasized the fact that an individual was not alone but rather an integral part of a larger community that extended both backward and forward in time, and they also served to connect groups that might be separated by space.

Most of our ancestors utilized ceremony and ritual in every aspect of their lives. There were purification ceremonies to be performed when taboos were broken. There were planting rituals, ceremonies to bring rain, thanksgiving rituals for the harvest, hunting rituals, even eating rituals. Ceremonies were performed to celebrate personal events, such as recovery from a serious illness, moving into a new house, or completing a dangerous journey. Performing these rituals offered a way of showing honor and respect for the divine aspects that are present in ordinary life. They gave people a way of marking their triumphs as well as their defeats and of filling these life passages, both large and small, with their proper significance.

Modern people experience a profound sense of loss over the lack of genuine ritual in their lives. One of the ways this lack is illustrated is through the ways in which young people attempt to carve out coming-of-age rituals for themselves. Lacking the time-honored, traditional ceremonies for marking their transitions into adulthood, young people now try to simulate these experiences through hazing at colleges (initiation into a college fraternity by exacting humiliating deeds), self-rendered initiation into gang families, and through sports-team bonding. None of these substitutes offers much emotional or spiritual satisfaction, and neither do they give the participants a deep sense of belonging to the larger community. In fact, while participants in these activities tend to feel a great sense of kinship with one another, their membership in these groups usually alienates them from a sense of belonging to those outside the group.

Rituals appeal to our psyche because they give form to the formless. They allow us to enter into the great mystery of the universe and help us step beyond the normal parameters of life. They can also help us to mend many emotional wounds, ranging from the loss of a loved one to the wound of raw anger in response to grievance. Sometimes emotions can be too intense to be controlled through an act of will. Uncontrolled, they may escalate into aggressive behavior or violence. Rituals can provide a safe means of releasing these intense emotions. It may also be that some of our obsessive-compulsive behaviors, addictions, and discontent are the result of the absence of ceremony and ritual in our lives.

Rituals signify beginnings and endings and are effective for emotional healing. A girl, describing her rape experience, talked about a cleansing ritual that was performed with her friends at the site of the rape as a way of coming to terms with the experience. She said, "Rituals are a wonderful way of drawing a box around something so you can begin to let go of it."[3]

Having a ritualized form of expression for the extremes of human emotion helps to contain and clarify the experience. It offers a safe alternative to inappropriate expression. It can also offer a way of expiating guilt for wrongs committed. For example, in some cultures, when someone has committed an act that violates the code of the culture, rather than be overwhelmed with guilt and self-sabotage, the individual can perform a ritualized penance. These kinds of rituals acknowledge the darker side of human nature and offer ways of integrating these tendencies and emotions into the culture so that everyone benefits and feels connected.

Another function of ceremony is as a form of worship. By performing rituals and carrying on traditions, you acknowledge and honor the creator of all life. Thus ritual provides a way of stepping out of ordinary reality and into sacred and spiritual realms. It creates an entrance point between the seen and unseen realms.

There are many kinds of rituals, ranging from those that are thousands of years old and celebrated by large masses of people to some that may be private and spontaneous, such as lighting a single candle and sitting quietly for a few moments. Although ceremonies and traditions vary widely throughout the world, there are some aspects that are common to all of them. Ritual involves taking time to understand how a certain facet of one's experience fits into the larger context of life. Ceremonies, traditions, and rituals act to put life's experiences in accord with the dictates of nature and the greater panorama of life. It is an act of power to revive old traditions and rituals.

Reviving Old Rituals

There are many ways of reviving old rituals and finding out about forgotten ceremonies and traditions. You can do research in your public library. You can talk to your older relatives and elderly people in general to see what kinds of rituals may have been practiced when they were young.

Once you have found out what the old traditions of your ancestors were, you can think about ways to incorporate them into your life now. It is likely that some of these rituals will appeal to you, while others will not have meaning for you or may not be in accordance with your values. Take what works for you, and ignore the rest. If your ancestors sacrificed a lamb every spring, you might not want to do this. However, after considering the spirit behind this practice, you might decide that every spring you would like to give something of value to the community. Ancient rituals can often be adapted to modern times. The way in which that spirit is expressed is not the most important thing; it is the spirit of the ritual that is valuable.

HOW DO YOU DECIDE WHICH HERITAGE RITUALS TO USE?

Many people in our modern world do not come from only one ethnic heritage but can claim membership in several different groups. If that is the case for you, then research the various ethnic strains that compose your heritage. When you have finished, you can choose which of the old rituals and traditions feel right for you to use in your life now.

For example, Carmen was of Irish and Mexican heritage. She was a baby boomer who had grown up in a typical American, suburban-sprawl neighborhood. The traditions celebrated by her family were not large in number and were very like those celebrated by others of their class in suburbia in the

1950s, such as making a wish when you blow out the candles on your birthday cake and getting drunk when you turn twenty-one. Carmen felt bereft over the lack of ceremonies with any deeper meaning or significance in her life, so she began to research the traditions of her ancestors. She felt an equal attraction to both the cultures that made up her heritage. Each seemed to reflect a different aspect of her personality and life, so she gathered information about both.

Because she felt a need for more sacred energy in her life, Carmen decided to use old Celtic ceremonies for honoring the four elements: air, water, fire, and earth. She also began to celebrate the annual Mexican Day of the Dead. She said that incorporating these ceremonies from her heritage into her present life made her feel much more complete and whole. They filled a great need in her life that before she had experienced as a sense of emptiness and as a lack of real connection to her roots.

WHAT IF YOU CANNOT TRACE YOUR ANCESTRY OR DO NOT FEEL CONNECTED TO YOUR HERITAGE?

Not all individuals feel a sense of connection with the traditions of their heritage, and some people are not sure exactly what their ancestry is. It is not necessary to research and utilize only the traditions of your blood heritage. Your heritage can also be what is in your heart. You might feel drawn to the ceremonies and traditions of a culture where you have lived or spent a great deal of time, in this life or another. Perhaps your family has had a strong attachment to the traditions of a particular culture. I have a friend in London who has completely immersed herself in Caribbean culture. She wears Caribbean-style clothes, listens to Caribbean music, and celebrates all the traditions, ceremonies, and rituals of that culture. Although she is of European descent, she speaks with a Caribbean accent, so I assumed she must have grown up in that part of the world. I was very surprised to learn that my friend was Austrian and had grown up in Vienna. Perhaps a past-life memory led her to make the choices she has, or maybe it is only that the Caribbean culture and traditions feed her soul in a way that her own culture cannot.

Take some time to examine your relationship to your roots and your culture. Are you drawn to the traditions of another culture because you are denying your own roots? Or do another culture's traditions meet your needs in a way that your own do not? Does another culture seem familiar to you, almost as though it were activating ancient memories from another lifetime? Before you adopt another culture's traditions think about your reasons for doing so. When you are clear in your heart and soul about your motivation, then proceed.

RESIDUAL MEMORIES FROM YOUR HERITAGE

One of Janet's grandparents had been Hopi, but she had grown up in New York City and didn't know anything about the Hopi Indian heritage. She married when she was twenty-three and had a child several years later in a home birth. When the child was born, she was asked for a name, and none was forthcoming. With the passing days, friends and family became more insistent that she must name her child. She replied that it didn't feel right to name the child so soon after birth. She was as surprised as others at her response. Twenty days after the birth, she invited friends and family over for a spontaneous naming ceremony for the child.

Later, when Janet was in her mid-forties, she researched her Hopi heritage and was surprised to find that, in Hopi tradition, when a child is born, it has no name for the first twenty days of its life. Then on the twentieth day, there is a ceremony where the child is presented to the sun and given its name.

Perhaps knowledge of the Hopi naming ritual resided in Janet's ancestral memories. She said she wished she had known about the ceremonies of her heritage earlier as it would have helped her to make sense of her desire to delay naming her child and would have helped her to create a naming ceremony.

Creating New Rituals and Traditions

We all have an inherent ability to create and enact ceremonies in our lives that are transformational and empowering. Although many ceremonies of the past were officiated by a priest or holy person, it is not necessary always to use a mediator between the human realm and the realm of spirit. You have within yourself a place that is holy and sacred, an inner sage. You can access your inner wisdom and intuition when you create your own rituals for the new millennium.

Some valuable rituals to create for yourself or your family members are rite-of-passage ceremonies. These kinds of ceremonies mark the end of one phase of life and initiate us into who we are becoming. It is important to honor these passages as a way of acknowledging our journey through life. Rites of passage pay homage to the cosmic relationship between human beings and the natural world. They allow us to experience our connections to the rhythms of the universe.

When my daughter, Meadow, graduated from high school, the mother of one of her friends decided to host an afternoon of celebration and ceremony for the mothers and graduating daughters. Food was shared around a huge table. After eating, one by one, each mother presented her daughter with a box that had within it items that represented the young woman's childhood, as well as items that represented the mother's wishes for her daughter in the future. It was a powerful time of passage for both the mothers and daughters.

Rite-of-passage ceremonies can also be created for children at the age of puberty. I heard of a group of friends who decided that they wanted to create rites of passage for their children to experience when they entered into adulthood. They wanted each child to understand what it would mean to be an adult and what this new role would entail in society. Over the years, each of their children participated in the ceremony that they created. Their rite of passage was performed when a boy reached thirteen and when a girl reached her first menses.

In this rite, friends and family members of the same sex gather together on an appointed evening for the ceremony, which continues until the next day. A mother presides over a girl's ceremony, and a father presides over a boy's rite. As part of the ceremony, each adult participant asks the child a prepared question and engages him or her in dialogue. Questions such as "What do you see as your future role in society?" and "What are your primary values and beliefs?" are asked of the child. During the dialogue that follows these questions, the adults are able to share with the children what it is like to be an adult. Often deep and heartfelt emotions are shared. At the completion of the dialogue time, the child spends the night alone in nature.

The next morning, the child is expected to offer some service of benefit to all, such as baking bread for everyone. Then friends and family of both sexes gather together to share the food prepared by the child. The meal is followed by a naming ceremony, where the child receives his or her spiritual name, which may be the same as the birth name.

The naming ceremony is followed by the adoption of a godmother or godfather. This adult promises to be supportive of the child throughout the child's life and act as a guardian in times of need. Then the godparent gives a gift to the child. After this gift-giving, each member of the community gives a meaningful gift, either a tangible gift or a song or a poem or even a single remark, and these are recorded in a beautiful journal that is given to the child to cherish for life. At the conclusion of the gift-giving, there is a feast and celebration.

This beautiful and moving ceremony is one example of how one group of people created a new tradition to meet their needs. It can be used as a prototype for anyone who wants to create a ceremony for a rite of passage or to commemorate a child's entrance into adulthood. When creating a ceremony, you can design the details to meet your own needs and the needs of the occasion you wish to celebrate. Some events that you might want to create rituals for may include the birth of a child, birthdays, a daughter's first menses, a son's entrance into manhood, graduation, marriage, completion of a difficult task, a new job, overcoming a fear, divorce, moving to a new home, separation from a loved one, the return of a loved one, getting over illness or injury, menopause, and the death of a loved one.

When you are creating new traditions and rituals, spend time carefully planning each aspect. Make sure, if there are other people involved, that they understand what their roles will be. But remember, even if things don't go completely according to your plans, don't get upset. Just let it go. It is the energy beneath the form that carries the power in ritual. The form that you choose simply allows you to focus your intent.

The most important aspect of any ceremony is your intention. Take time to become very clear about your intent for the ritual. In other words, what results do you want from your ceremony? Once you are clear about your intention, then the details of the ritual will fall into place and you will be led in the direction you desire. Without clear intent, a ritual can become a hollow and meaningless form.

NEW RITUALS FOR HOLIDAYS AND SEASONS

Rituals are a structure within which our unconscious can focus to honor beginnings and endings. In ancient times, holidays (which comes from the words *holy day*) and the passing of each season were honored with ceremonies. For example, according to historians, long before the birth of Christ, most cultures had a winter celebration or a solstice ritual. People who lived close to the earth equated the sun and light with life. They understood the spiritual energy that occurred at the time of the solstice. In accordance with their beliefs, they offered gifts to the Creator requesting the return of the sun and light. The winter celebration was sacred; it was a time of honoring the great cycle of life. For the most part, in modern culture, we have lost the spiritual significance of this holy event. Many people in Western cultures now associate this special time with the birth of Christ, but the sacredness of even this event has been lost to commercialism and consumerism.

When creating ceremonies for holidays and seasons, you may want to incorporate traditional rituals as well as trusting your intuition for ideas. It is important that you look for the underlying energy beneath each ceremony. For example, underlying a spring ceremony is the idea of new beginnings. When creating a new tradition for spring, you might want to include eggs in your ceremony as being symbolic of new things that you wish to give birth to in your life. In ancient spring ceremonies, eggs were used in this manner, a custom adopted by Christianity for the Easter festival.

CEREMONIALLY HONORING ANCESTORS

In many cultures, days are set aside during the year to honor one's ancestors, or historical and cultural heroes. For example, in some countries, Veterans Day or Remembrance Day is honored as a way of paying tribute to those who have served in war or who have died in battle. If there are people in your family or your ancestry who are veterans of war or who have died in battle, creating a ritual to honor them and to remember their deeds can bring a deeper understanding of the valor of those individuals.

One of the most moving ceremonies I ever attended was a Jewish remembrance ceremony. The ceremony was held in

Amsterdam on a chilly evening in an open-air building. The building had been a holding place for Dutch Jews before they were shipped off to concentration camps in the Second World War. (The Netherlands had the highest percentage of Jewish people per country who were killed during the war.) A solemn and sacred feeling enveloped us as the names of the death camps were sung slowly and deliberately. It was a time to remember those who had died. I sat between two people who had survived the concentration camps and had lost many family members. I could sense the deep comfort and immense power they got from being part of such a profound ceremony.

You can also create a ritual for prayers for peace for future generations. Rituals of this kind can be a way of directing energy and vital life forces. They can be used as a focal point to magnify intention and move energy into form. Using a ritual for your prayers for peace can genuinely generate an energy that radiates into the world.

Some cultures have ceremonies to honor ancestors and those who have passed on. There is value in doing this. It expands our cultural sense of continuum and it honors death as one of the fundamental transitions in life. A holiday celebrated in some Latin countries is the Day of the Dead, a day set aside to honor those who have died. Our culture has an interesting perspective about death; basically, as a culture we deny death. Death embarrasses us, and those who are dying often enter into the ranks of the untouchables. In most ancient cultures, death was understood as an important aspect of life, and it was given a noble place in society. When my daughter's school decided to give the children an understanding of the various holidays from around the world, one of the holidays that they celebrated was the Day of the Dead. Unfortunately, someone in the press heard that schoolchildren were celebrating the Day of the Dead, and the school got negative media coverage for exposing the children to a so-called macabre holiday, which, in fact, is a very compassionate holiday.

MYTHS AND STORIES

Along with rituals, myths are one of the most important means of imparting the values of a culture to one's descendants. Myths provide us with universal images and symbols that have been passed down through the generations and that have universal significance. Myths tell the stories of heroes who have gone before us, paving the way for us so that we don't have to venture into the unknown alone. They provide us with the sense that the labyrinth of the future has already been traveled by voyagers from the past. They offer us hope that we, too, can find our way through, for the journey repeats itself over and over again throughout time. Acquainting yourself with the stories and myths of the past lights your pathway into the future and beyond. Joseph Campbell wrote: "It has been the chief function of much of mythological lore . . . to carry . . . the individual across the critical thresholds from infancy to adulthood, and from old age to death."[4]

In ancient cultures, mythology formed a foundation for life. It created a structure within which the spontaneous emerging of the human spirit could be formulated. It functioned as a kind of transition point between the unknown and the known, between the mysterious and the visible form.

Myths are not just whimsical stories. They are a part of a vast inner universe that creates a structure against which all experience is measured. They provide us with an anchor to which we can secure our lives. They can point us toward our destinies. Mythology fills the deep need of the human spirit to identify with something larger than itself, to identify with the mysterious and the cosmic. Without this, life's experiences can seem mundane and insignificant.

A society depends on mythology to offer a sense of cohesion. Cultural myths can weld disparate groups together and provide people with a common vision. Part of the discontent and confusion of our present world may stem from a lack of relevant myths, because myths serve to unify our experiences and give us a premise for interpreting the realities of our lives. Without a coherent system of mythology, our experiences can seem disjointed and meaningless.

Personal Myths

There can be tremendous value in examining the myths that underlie your perceptions of reality. Our personal myths are made up, in part, of the myths shared by our culture, but also of the myths embraced by our families and the stories that we make up ourselves to explain the experiences we have had. Every person is a storyteller, even if he or she does not recognize this. We all take the experiences of our lives and string them together into a story that makes sense. In the telling of our lives, we minimize some parts and elaborate on others. Every family has many stories that they tell and retell. These stories define their identity. So, too, do *our personal myths define what we believe and who we are.* They contribute to our ultimate destinies.

Personal myths are a psychological framework that gives dignity and understanding to all the circumstances of your life. They are the context within which your story is understood. Personal myths allow us to interface with our psyche in a way that gives meaning to even the smallest aspects of our lives. They are also a way that the inner workings of our souls can express themselves through images, symbols, feelings, and intuitions.

Exploring your personal myths allows you to access the deeper wisdom that resides inside you. It can help you to deal with personal dilemmas, emotional turmoil, and recurring patterns by revealing the context of meaning in which these problems exist. Discovering your personal myths can provide a sense of understanding as an antidote to the meaninglessness that has plagued our time.

When you explore your personal mythology, you become more in touch with your individual and collective origins. When you are unaware of what myths underlie your assumptions about reality, you do not have the power to change them. This is why learning about your personal myths is such a powerful exercise.

PERSONAL MYTHS BRING A COHESION AND MEANING TO LIFE

Though you may like to think of yourself as a unified identity, in fact, your personality is made up of multiple aspects. Beneath your tranquil exterior, there exists a multitude of personal qualities. Although you may exemplify one particular attribute fixed over time, there are a number of other qualities waiting beneath the surface. For example, on the surface you may seem to be a caring mother, wife, lover, child, and friend, but there are touches of the harlot, the villain, the hero, the goddess, and the wild woman that also lurk deep within your soul. You contain within yourself an entire range of human possibilities. Myths can help you to understand and unify these aspects of self. Inner stability is achieved when you accept and find room for all these parts in your life. Discovering your personal mythology is one way of incorporating the various parts of your personality into a whole.

Your personal myths can provide you with a structure for interpreting your life, a kind of lens that you can observe your life through. This does not mean putting on rose-colored glasses and creating a false portrayal of yourself. Rather, it means sorting out the threads of meaning from all your experiences and weaving them together into a coherent view of your whole life.

Your personal myths are a template through which you can organize your perceptions, experiences, and actions. They acknowledge that you are the distillation point of a long lineage. Whether you are aware of them or not, you are living your mythology. However, when you become conscious of your beliefs and the significance they have on what you are becoming, then you are able to make the changes that will allow you to live passionately and freely. You will be aware of the choices that you make and their significance. Sorting through your personal mythology can help you to weld your outer circumstances to their inner meanings, thus creating a cohesive whole, and this, in turn, can have value for your descendants.

WRITING YOUR PERSONAL MYTHS

To understand your personal myths you need to step back from your life and see it within its greater context. You must discover the forces that have motivated your life and see where your destiny is leading you. One very valuable tool for doing this is to write your own autobiography. You do not have to be a writer to do this. Nor do you need to think that you have a particularly interesting story to tell. Everyone's autobiography is unique and wonderful. By taking the time to write your story, you will discover the truth of this, regardless of what your assumptions were before you began.

It can be helpful to organize your life story around themes. Rather than writing a sequence of events, such as "first I did this, and then I did this," and so on, try thinking in mythological terms. What are the dragons that you have had to slay? You are the hero of your own story. You may be a reluctant hero, a shy hero, or perhaps a very imperfect hero, but you are a hero nevertheless. In folklore the hero sets forth from ordinary life into the mystical realms, where he encounters villains and helping spirits. There are battles to be won and forces of darkness to be overcome. When he returns from his quest, the hero carries wisdom gained from all that he has experienced.

What forces of darkness have you encountered in your life? Who were the angels and spiritual assistants who helped guide your way? What or who have been the villains in your life? Who have been the wise ones? What battles have you won? What battles have you lost? When did evil forces make you lose your way? What were your triumphs? What wisdom have you gained? What have you learned? What have you gifted to others? What are the pivotal events of your life? When did your childhood end? What marked your entrance into adulthood? Who have been key people in your life? If your life had a moral, what would it be?

Even if it is hard or uncomfortable, the act of writing your autobiography can have a powerful impact on your life. It will allow you to view your life in perspective, and it also will offer a legacy for those who follow you (see chapter 4 regarding passing down your story to your descendants).

You don't have to write about your entire life. You can choose portions of your life that were the most meaningful to you and write about them. It need not be a gothic novel. Your myth might be short and sweet, like a children's story. When you write your story, notice what you choose to expand on, what you choose to leave out, and why. The process of choosing what to write about is as powerful as the actual writing.

There are a number of ways in which you can write your story. You might choose to use a myth form with heroes and villains, gods and goddesses, illustrating the different aspects of your life. Or you might want to write short vignettes that represent the different stages of your life. You can use chapters to delineate different phases of your life, or you may want to choose a theme of your life and write about incidents that illustrate it.

The past is as malleable as the future, and it is constantly evolving. Your myths and stories about your past change as you change. Creating your autobiography offers a structure for understanding where you have come from and how you have come to be who you are. The act of writing all this down can sometimes change your point of view about events and people.

When you take the time to sit down and go through all your memories, you may discover that your view of how your favorite aunt, Sally, forgot your birthday when you were ten has changed considerably over the years. Back then, you felt that she had betrayed you and perhaps no longer loved you. As a woman of forty, you realize that she was going through a divorce at the time and was in too much pain to be aware of others' needs. This is one example of how the past can change just through the action of reviewing it from another perspective.

When you have completed your story, see if there is a particular track that your myth takes. For instance, is there a theme of sadness, or anger, or sweetness and light throughout your myth? Do you want this track, or would you rather choose another one? You may choose to keep the track of your particular myth, or you can choose to rewrite your story using another pathway. The way you view your past can make a difference to your future.

In writing your story, you will also become aware of how your personal story both converges and diverges from the larger myths of your culture, for no man is an island. We are all co-creating life on our planet, and by becoming clear about your own personal myths, you are helping to create the larger, cultural myth in a more cohesive, positive way.

CREATING A LEGACY STORY

There is tremendous value in writing your autobiography for your eyes only, so that you can be completely honest in your feelings. By keeping your story private, you are free to say whatever you want and make sense of your life in this way, without having to worry about hurting anyone's feelings. However, once you have completed this process, you may want to edit some or all of your story and create a new story that you can share with your descendants. I call doing this creating a legacy story. It is a wonderful gift that you can share with those who will come after you.

When you are writing something for others to read, it is important to consider both their feelings and your purpose in sharing your writing with them. When you are creating a legacy story, there are a number of decisions to be made. There is no single right way of telling the truth. Your personal history can be presented in many ways. Do you want your story to be a living monument to the good character you possessed and to what you achieved in your life, or do you want to be unabashedly honest and reveal all aspects of your life, good and bad? In order to answer this question, you need to be clear as to your intentions.

There is a wonderful feeling associated with presenting a legacy story that is filled with courage and triumph. This makes you feel good and will make your descendants proud of you, their ancestor. Not many people would be comfortable knowing, for example, that their ancestors were liars or thieves. By writing your legacy story in a way that is bright and bold, you have the additional advantage of producing a story that you will want to live up to. What is expected tends to be realized. When others think the very best of us, we tend to manifest the best in ourselves. Your story can give those who follow you an example that is inspiring and beautiful.

Another way to write your legacy story is to reveal everything. Though perhaps uncomfortable for all concerned, there can be great value in writing down all aspects of your life, both the good and the bad, the honorable and the dishonorable. Writing about the mistakes in your life and the family secrets, which everyone knows and no one speaks about, can be healing for you and can offer understanding for those who follow you. For example, had I known growing up that my grandmother (on my father's side) silently suffered emotional abuse from her father-in-law (my great-grandfather), I would have had greater compassion for her while she was alive.

Or you might choose a middle path, revealing some things that are somewhat painful for you or others but choosing to keep other aspects of your story private. It is your choice, and there is power in the choosing. Whichever way you choose to create your legacy story has value. It is a very individual decision, and there is no right way.

Here are some excerpts from my legacy story as an example of one way to write your personal myths.

Introduction

I was scrawny and ugly when I was born. My father couldn't believe that a baby could look so ugly. I grew like a weed into a scrappy little thing, taking root wherever I could. We moved nine times, so my roots would go down, and then get ripped back up again. We never seemed to have enough money, and we were always on the move.

I knew how to fight. My knees and elbows were always scabbed over. I was the eldest of four kids and took it upon myself to be the defender of my brothers and sister whenever they got picked on as the new kids in town.

Chapter One: South Side, Chicago

The walls were thin in the small tenement apartment we lived in. The winter chill penetrated through the walls. The summer heat was stifling. The sounds of the elevated inner-city train shook the walls. We didn't live in a safe section of Chicago, and more than once I used my fists to protect my siblings.

I loved Thursdays; that was the day the junk man came around with his horse and cart. It was a glorious adventure, to scout through the alleys in the trash cans, looking for thrown-away treasures to sell to him. Most items earned a nickel or dime that we used to buy red licorice at the candy store. A perfectly good mug might fetch a nickel. I found a red lampshade once and earned thirty-five cents.

Chapter Two: Northfield, Chicago

We moved to a really nice neighborhood in a Chicago suburb. It was great. We had a two-story house with a lawn and even an apple tree. Best of all, next door lived a really nice boy my age. His name was David. One night, some men broke into David's house and he and his family were tied up and put in the crawl space beneath the house. Everyone was okay, but I realized that nice neighborhoods weren't everything they were cracked up to be.

Chapter Three: Ohio

Our next move found us living in a small town in a very conservative farming community in the Midwest. Here girls didn't fight to resolve differences. They cajoled and gossiped and whispered in low conspiratorial tones, but they didn't slug each other. They were supposed to grow up to be gentle wives and mothers. I didn't know how to fit in and make friends. Up to that point in life, making friends had never been my strong point.

One day as I sat alone on the long school bus ride home, I made a conscious decision to make friends in this new town. I didn't know quite how to do it, so I decided to study the kids who had friends and see what made them different. The next day at the school yard, I clandestinely observed the most popular girl at school, to see what she did differently from me. She was always smiling. Every time she did it, everyone around her seemed friendlier. I felt that I had discovered the secret of making friends: all I had to do was to smile a lot.

That night I locked myself in the bathroom and stood on my tiptoes to see in the mirror. I practiced turning up the corners of my mouth. It was a weird sensation; I wasn't used to smiling very much. It took a while to get it right. (In most of my early childhood photos I'm scowling.) Quite frankly, I thought smiling made my face look stupid. The next day in the playground, I contorted my mouth into the big smile shape. I felt a bit silly doing it, and I was worried that kids would laugh at me. I was amazed. Kids smiled back at me. It was like magic. I had discovered how to make friends. It was a long time later in life that I realized that people could like me for who I was. I didn't need always to be smiling and nice.

At home, dark and terrible things were happening behind closed doors—things that still haunt me to this day. I was eventually separated from my parents and sent to California to stay with my grandparents in the eastern section of Los Angeles.

Chapter Four: Los Angeles

The California sun was great. My grandparents loved me. And my ability to defend weaker kids wasn't a liability. Most of the girls at my new school sharpened their rattail combs to a fine point and stuck them in their beehive hairstyles, ready to use as a knife in the event of an attack. I never used my comb as a weapon, but it gave me a sense of security; although it must have looked ridiculous, having a comb sticking out of my head all the time.

Gramma was an astrologer and a bit of a mystic. She was convinced that I had "powers." She was strictly forbidden by my father to talk to me of such things, because he was a "man of science." But periodically she would drop her voice to a whisper, as if my father could hear, even though he was thousands of miles away, and talk to me about the spirit realm.

Chapter Five: The Midwest

After several years, I was reunited first with one parent for a while, and then with the other for my high-school years in another small farming community. Thus began the most difficult and challenging years of my life. Somehow I survived those years, but the scars still run deep. During that time, I saw my grandmother only a few times, but each time I saw her, she would whisper in my ear: "Everything that is happening to you is for a greater purpose, Denise." Gramma offered me hope and made me believe that there might be some value in all the things that I was going through in my life.

DECIDING WHAT YOU WANT TO INCLUDE IN YOUR LEGACY STORY

When I thought about what I wanted to include in my legacy story for my daughter, I decided to reveal both the highs and the lows of my life. Although there is a part of me that wants to leave a legacy for her that is grand and wondrous, instead I have chosen to tell her everything, not just my triumphs. My legacy story has my pain as well as my joy.

I have spent so much of my life trying to find my truth and facing the deeply disturbing and uncomfortable parts of myself and my life that I felt I owed it to myself and my descendants to present a legacy that was honest, yet compassionate, humorous, and loving. I aimed to be fair, and rather than hurt someone unduly or blame anyone needlessly, I've attempted to tell my story in a form that promotes understanding of the greater forces at play and the value I have gained from even the worst situations.

Hopefully, my legacy story will create a template for my descendants for candid inquiry into the hidden secrets that each family possesses. I've had too much pain concealed in my life to be less than open, and I hope my descendants will forgive any undue discomfort that my story may cause. This is the path I've chosen. Each individual needs to choose for herself.

Choosing how to present your story is not always an easy decision. The process of deciding the form that your story takes can be as powerful a process as actually writing your legacy. It may not be an easy or clear-cut decision for you, but your story is important and how you record it will offer value to those who follow you.

If it seems too overwhelming to make a myth of your entire life, then choose an aspect of your life. My friend Rebecca wrote me a letter telling me about a change in her relationship with Kathy, who is also my friend. She used a mythic form to communicate with me about the change. I found her letter moving and powerful. I've included parts of it here as an example of one way to write your personal life as a myth. The original letter was much longer and very beautifully presented.

> *Long ago, before there was time, two souls, declaring their love for each other, decided to meet again and again through time. Through the centuries they met, renewing vows of love, in different clothes and in different bodies.*
>
> *In the late part of the twentieth century, these two once again were inextricably drawn together as maidens from different lands. They recognized each other and knew deep inside that they were destined to be rejoined. They lived together on the gentle waters of a land born of fire. Inspired through their meetings with other ancient souls, these gentle maidens pioneered a project, a touchstone for themselves and others.*
>
> *From idea to fruition was but a moment in time. And then they journeyed to another land, a land even more ancient than the first, to create a place of refuge. As the seasons passed, they became aware that they were stewards of something majestic and wondrous, a touchstone for many that took on a life force of its own.*
>
> *But then the time came when the maidens knew that something was changing. Challenges appeared in their life,*

but their love ran so deep that they continued on their path together. However, a time of knowing evolved. They knew that their destinies would take them in different directions. But through the fears, wounds, and uncertainties of change, they also knew their love could still be strong and deep.

Each day became easier; it felt as if the entire universe of earth and the stars supported their willingness and courage to change. The future did not make itself totally clear, but the young maidens developed a trust in the wisdom of the Creator that sustained them. So now as the future unfolds, the maidens walk, day by day, night by night, season into season, with their paths still together, yet apart . . . fulfilling their ancient vows once again.

YOUR LEGACY STORY CAN CHANGE

Your mythic story can change. It is not set in the firmament. We are used to observing the world in one way. We believe that objects exist or they don't exist. We believe that the world is made up of solid, separate forms. Quantum mechanics declare that this is not so. Things are not always as they seem. Your story can change. Your past can change. Your view of the past can change. As you evolve and grow, so your past evolves and changes. Periodically, review your legacy story, and revise or rewrite it as needed.

Attempting to follow personal myths that are not in sync with who you are is like wearing a shoe that doesn't fit. You will find yourself constrained and contained. Mythology can be a bridge between meaning and experience, and if your personal myths don't fit, then your life will seem meaningless, because you won't be able to journey across the bridge to the deeper underlying meaning in all things.

We need to release the shackles of some of the old and outdated myths that limit our full potential. It is essential that we reach into the sacred inner realms and envisage a vast range of new myths—myths that were previously unimaginable. It is time to recognize and realign the myths that we adhere to, both our personal mythology and our cultural myths. Our mythology reaches into the wellspring of our psyche and points the way to the future. We are entering a time when we are less able to rely on the myths of our forebears, and we need to create myths and stories that can propel us into a future that is unlike anything that has ever been seen before.

New Myths and Stories for the Next Century

The approach of the new century and a new millennium is a remarkable time to create new stories and myths. Stories feed the soul and are essential for the psychological well-being of the generations that follow us. Many of the old stories told around tribal fires and passed down through generations have died. It is an act of power and hope to revive the ancient tradition of storytelling and even to create new stories that can be passed down. New stories can come in many ways. They can come spontaneously when we tell bedtime stories to our children, they can come on vacations as we sit around a campfire, and they can come gently on the wings of dreams. My father enjoys creating stories. Here is one of his stories that he shared with me when I was a child. It's a good story for the next century.

A long time ago, there was a young man who set out to seek his fortune. He went in search of the gold at the end of the rainbow. One day on his journey, he saw a huge rainbow splashed from one end of the sky to the other. He ran and found the end of the rainbow in an overgrown old apple orchard. The orchard was part of a large property owned by an old woman. The young man didn't have any money, but he went to the old woman and offered to exchange his labor for her abandoned orchard. The old woman was more than happy to trade, because she needed the labor and the apple orchard was useless. Nothing grew well on that plot of land.

The young man worked hard during the day, but late every afternoon, he would dig in the orchard, hoping to find the pot of gold. Neighbors would stop by and ask him why he was digging. Not wanting to tell them about the gold, he replied, "I'm digging a root cellar." Of course, he eventually had to build a root cellar so people wouldn't be suspicious.

A curious thing began to happen to the orchard. Suddenly, new life came into the trees, and plump red apples hung from the trees. This happened because as the young man dug, he made holes in the hardpan soil so that proper drainage could occur and the trees' roots were able to go deeper. He continued to dig every evening, and when people asked him why he was digging, he did not want them to find out about the gold, so he said, "I'm digging a foundation for a barn." Not wanting people to be suspicious, he took the profit from his apples and built a barn. After a few years, he had a fine house, a barn, a root cellar, and a number of other buildings, a glorious orchard—and a wife *and children. He never stopped looking for the gold, and every evening would find him digging on his land. Years passed by, and the young man grew to be an old man. Late one afternoon, as he sat on the porch of his home, looking across the apple orchard, he saw his granddaughter running through the grass. Her hair was shining and golden in the lingering light of the sun.*

He smiled and thought, I have found my gold at the end of the rainbow.

New Ceremonies, Rituals, and Traditions for the Next Century

Our descendants will hold this period in history with reverence. Grandchildren will talk about what their grandparents did for the beginning of the new century. Taking the time to plan now for the beginning of a new millennium will allow an energy to build until that time. You can begin to plan ahead for the twenty-first century by asking yourself the questions, "Where will I be? What does this time represent to me? What ceremonies can I create that will mark my entrance into a new time period? Who do I wish to be present with me?" The universe listens to symbolic gestures. The new traditions and rituals that you create for the new century can be woven out of your greatest hopes for the future. They can help heal our deepest fears for the years ahead. They raise our sights toward all the best that we can be, even as they remind us not to become the worst that we can imagine, as we step with strength and glory into a new planetary beginning.

6

Gateway to the Future

SPIRITUAL AWAKENING OR APOCALYPSE? THE CHOICE IS OURS

At this moment, we stand at the advent of the most exciting time in the history of our planet. We hold in our hands the opportunity to shape planetary destiny through our actions, our thoughts, and our expectations. The potential for momentous change has never been greater, and the accompanying responsibility can feel overwhelming. There is no doubt the challenges facing us are real. The problems that threaten the well-being of our species and the entire planet are large and immediate. The news media daily present us with information that is both frightening and true. Pollution, wars, terrorist attacks, the decimation of endangered lands and animals—we are constantly confronted with evidence of current and impending crises. They make our fears about these threats completely understandable. However, less frequently are we reminded of the efforts that are being made to turn the tide of despair—the large and small successes that are also occurring. It is important to honor these successes, because they encourage faith and belief in the future *and our beliefs will be a powerful force in determining whether we move forward into a bright future or one filled with global devastation.*

It is easy to give way to the onslaught of discouraging facts and slide into fear, apathy, and inaction. But these attitudes, although understandable, are a luxury we can no longer afford. What is expected tends to be realized, and what we expect about the future can become a self-fulfilling prophesy. Do you expect monumental earth changes, such as earthquakes and torrential storms, as we step into the next century?

What are your personal expectations and beliefs about the future? Do you believe a cataclysm is inevitable? Do you imagine that your descendants will continue, generation after generation, learning, loving, and creating a better world for those who will follow them? We must confront our own fears and trace their roots in order to shift them into a more positive direction at a basic level.

THE APPEAL OF A CATACLYSM

If you believe that the future will be dark and that difficult changes are inevitably coming, you are not alone. The idea of an impending apocalypse is gaining popularity in groups as divergent as right-wing survivalists, born-again Christians, New Age adherents, and radical environmentalists. There is a certain horrific appeal to the idea of an imminent cataclysm, and there are a number of reasons why it is gaining popularity.

If you believe a cataclysm is coming, there can be great value in examining your inner motivations for thinking this way.

For some people, believing in an impending disaster allows them to feel a sense of being a part of something bigger than normal life. We all have a deep unquenchable desire for mystery and awe. We yearn for a transcendental or peak experience, where we become part of the majesty of the universe. But most of our lives are filled with paying the rent, getting to work on time, and a myriad of everyday details. Believing that we are a part of a magical and awesome time, a time when the destiny of humankind lies in the balance, provides a sense of exhilaration and purpose that many of our current religious and philosophical systems don't ignite. Believing that there is something special about our time and our place in the universe gives us a sense of being alive. Even if the images of disaster are hugely negative, for some people this time provides them with a larger context and a deeper meaning for their fears.

Many people who have a fascination with coming disaster harbor the belief that they can survive, even though most others will die. Some have moved from beautiful homes in Sydney, Australia, to the inland Blue Mountains because they believe that a huge tidal wave is going to wipe out Sydney. People have moved to Oregon from California because of predictions that the latter is going to fall into the sea. I also know those who are stockpiling food *and weapons*, because they believe that when the earth changes come, there will be worldwide chaos and they will need to defend their food and lives.

Although these beliefs perhaps have their source in feeling a part of something exhilarating and bigger than life, they can be dangerous because they support the idea that one should work to ensure the survival of friends and family, even to the detriment of everyone else. Although the ancient tribal instinct to support one's own tribe and fight other tribes may be a relic from our past, resisting this force is essential to the creation of a more tolerant world. For humanity to move forward peacefully into the twenty-first century, we need to work to change these tendencies in ourselves and in our culture.

Perhaps the allure of a worldwide cataclysm has its roots in the realm of myth. Because of the fatalistic nature and enormous impact of mass communication, we are constantly being assailed with information about the potential for cataclysmic changes in the world, which generates a cultural collective unconscious fear about our perilous times. Myths give form to the formless. They provide us with a means of interpreting things that are too large or overwhelming to think about in ordinary terms. In order to give form to our nebulous fears, perhaps we have collectively created a myth of the world coming to an end. This Armageddon myth provides us with a specific form to which we can attach our overwhelming and formless fears. I call the idea that we may encounter a cataclysm, as we enter into a new century and beyond, the Millennium Myth.

The Millennium Myth gives us a dragon to slay. To save us from this potential disaster, we look for a knight in shining armor in one form or another. One such potential solution embraced by Christians is the second coming of Christ. For a New Ager, the savior knight might be an inward evolution toward the spiritual awakening. The Millennium Myth attaches fear to a particular time rather than allowing it to remain in an indefinite and uncertain future. It helps replace the collective gnawing anxiety about our future with a certainty that we can each take action to avert potential disasters. The myth empowers us to be our best and gives form to our fears.

Another reason why the belief in a cataclysm has such a magnetic draw is because of the inherent desire in the human psyche to honor beginnings and endings. We honor New Year's Day, for it symbolically represents an ending and a new beginning. We celebrate our thirtieth, fortieth, and fiftieth birthdays, and so on, because each marks the completion of one decade and the beginning of the next. We are eternally striving to initiate new beginnings. In the search for meaning, most of our ancestors embraced rituals that celebrated beginnings and endings; these were considered sacred times. As most of the ancient rituals have been lost, perhaps as a species we yearn for a sense of completion and a desire to honor new beginnings. Perhaps images of a cataclysmic change followed by a new beginning for the earth fill this collective need.

New beginnings can also be symbolic of the death of sin and the rebirth of innocence. In the traditions of many religions, through penance we can begin anew. We confess our sins so we can be cleansed. Because human beings have a tendency to project onto the world deeper individual issues of the soul, belief in a cataclysmic earth-renewal may fulfill the need of our collective unconscious psyche to wash away societal sins of pollution and disrespect for the earth.

The appeal of endings and new beginnings has accompanied the end of every century. It is as if the year magically reverting to zero again marks a turning point in life. Throughout history, many end-of-the-world predictions have been based around the turn of a century. Perhaps these predictions reflect our desire to achieve fully the new beginning, which the turn of a century represents. But although the end of each century has often been full of prophets and soothsayers declaring the end of the world, the world has always managed to survive.

PSYCHIC PREDICTIONS REGARDING THE FUTURE

There have always been predictions of worldwide cataclysms, but none of them has come to fruition. At the turn of the last millennium, in the year 999, European society was full of predictions of doom. They thought it signified an ending of the world as they knew it. Fortunately, life went on. Some religions have been based on the idea that the world would end on a specific date, dates that have come and gone uneventfully.

During my research for this book, I became curious about the accuracy of previous psychic predictions of planetary changes. In surveying numerous predictions made thirty years ago, I couldn't find any that were consistently accurate. For example, in 1970, one famous New York psychic predicted that there would be a tremendous earthquake in 1974–75. He stated that this upheaval would devastate one-third of the world, including the United States, and that worldwide famine would result. The imprecision of his prediction is not unusual. Predictions such as those that the East Coast and/ or the West Coast of the United States will be submerged under water, or that there will be 1,000-foot tidal waves, pole shifts, and worldwide famine, have thus far proved false. Even the predictions regarding natural disasters made through the

British Premonitions Bureau, which opened in January 1967, and the Central Premonitions Registry in New York, which opened in 1968, have turned out to be inaccurate. There is no reason to believe that predictions being made now will turn out to be any more reliable than those from the past.

A problem common to most psychic predictions is that they are accurate only in retrospect. Even the remarkable accuracy of Nostradamus's predictions have been proved true only in this way. When I researched various individual interpretations of the Nostradamus quatrains, they were wildly disparate and inaccurate in their predictions of the future. However, in retrospect, present-day soothsayers were able successfully to dovetail Nostradamus's predictions with past world events. In 1987, a major publisher came out with the definitive guide to Nostradamus's predictions for the future and the millennium. Authored by a respected psychic, this book stated that Nostradamus predicted that by the mid-1990s East Africa would be split in three pieces, that New York and Florida would be flooded with water, and that the United States would be broken apart. This has yet to come. The author further stated that Nostradamus said that in July 1999 a holocaust will begin the final destruction of the civilized world and Easter Day in the year 2000 would mark great flooding in England and the southern part of England would sink beneath the sea. Although these dates have yet to come, I feel it is likely that these interpretations of Nostradamus will be as inaccurate as the others.

I have been fortunate to meet some remarkable psychics in my travels, and yet I have never met anyone who is one hundred percent correct. Every age has prophets and those who can see into the future. Even ordinary people can recount psychic perceptions, premonitions, or dreams that came true. Although in retrospect there are many predictions that have proved to be true, it is difficult and even impossible to know exactly which ones will come to fruition.

Many psychics have chosen the year 2000 for their premonitions of disasters, but it is interesting to note that while this year is the focus for many such prophecies, it may not necessarily be a remarkable date. In fact, the year 2000 is actually an arbitrary date, because most biblical scholars believe that Christ wasn't actually born in the year zero. Although Western cultures adhere to the Gregorian calendar, the year 2000 isn't necessarily recognized as a special turning point in cultures that do not monitor time using this system.

SCIENTIFIC PREDICTIONS REGARDING THE FUTURE

The predictions of scientists are not always any more remarkable than psychics' prophecies regarding the future. Science can very accurately indicate trends and probabilities, but it is impossible for a scientist to predict accurately events in the future that are basically unpredictable. For example, in the early nineteenth century, Thomas Malthus, a respected political economist, made a prediction of world collapse based on the surge in population that occurred in the late eighteenth century. His opinion was widely accepted at the time. He hypothesized that the world's population would outstrip its ability to produce food, thus causing world chaos. He was accurate in his assessment that the world's population would grow exponentially; however, he didn't foresee the concurrent advance in agricultural technology. Malthus's prediction was accurate for the information he had at the time. But all too often it is difficult to make accurate predictions because of unforeseen future circumstances.

In more recent time, the predictions of the famous Club of Rome study proved to be spectacularly wrong. In this study from the 1970s, world-class scientists projected that we would reach a complete collapse of civilization by the 1990s because of starvation generated by the population explosion. This dismal prediction was perhaps allayed by the green revolution, in which third-world countries were shown how to triple crop production through rotation and hybridization.

Many times scientists have made predictions about ecological collapse that have not been accurate. This doesn't necessarily mean that present predictions won't come true. It does mean that there are variables in any scientific prediction for the future. *This is a basis for hope!*

SCIENTIFIC HOPE FOR THE FUTURE

The very real potential for environmental disasters on our planet is often used to justify beliefs in a coming apocalypse. However, in spite of these environmental challenges, hope rises on the horizon. There has been an enormous change in consciousness worldwide over the past twenty-five years regarding the necessity of finding solutions to the threats to our ecological integrity, and as a result, new solutions to what were seemingly insoluble problems are being found.

The way in which the worldwide community has taken action on fluorocarbons is one example of this kind of thinking, and it encourages optimism for the future. Fluorocarbons, which are chemicals released by refrigeration units and aerosol cans, destroy ozone, the part of our atmosphere that protects us from harmful radiation. Not long ago, scientists realized that if the destruction of the ozone layer by fluorocarbons wasn't halted, there would be irreversible catastrophes on a global scale. Not only would cancer rates skyrocket, perhaps to the point where we would need to wear radiation suits outdoors, but also many plants and animals intolerant of radiation would die, thus causing a devastating chain reaction in the field of agriculture.

As a result of the consensus of opinion about the threat posed by fluorocarbons, representatives of the entire world came together in 1987 to sign the Montreal Protocol, banning the production of fluorocarbons. This was the first time in history that a global agreement was made that changed worldwide behavior in such a short space of time. During the Protocol debates, various spokesmen for fluorocarbon manufacturers said it would be useless to expect industry to find a replacement for fluorocarbons anytime in the future. However, the great news is that substitute technology has already been developed in the years since the proclamation. The actions taken as a result of the Montreal Protocol have ensured that the ozone layer will not be completely destroyed. It will take fifty to a hundred years for it to begin to return to normal, but the recovery phase has already begun.

Other challenging environmental problems are also facing our planet at this point in time, such as the phenomenon of global warming. This is a much more difficult problem to deal with than ozone destruction, because there seems to be no practical solution. However, even as scientific knowledge continues to expand exponentially in all other areas, so, too, is there significant evidence that solutions can and will be found for the environmental problems confronting us as well. What we as individuals can do to help this process is to educate ourselves about the problems (rather than ignoring them and hoping that this will make them go away), and then to make whatever personal choices we can to further the cause of finding solutions. This could take the form of changing our buying habits, donating money to research, or writing to legislators. No action is too small to make a difference, and as in the case of coming up with an alternative to fluorocarbons, the impasse we are facing today may be completely resolved in our lifetimes. Having hope and working together toward these goals is a powerful means for making them a reality.

As the population of our planet continues to grow, it becomes more and more imperative that we find ways of dealing creatively with the strains this places on our natural resources. One ray of hope regarding the ecology of the future was represented by the 1992 Earth Summit in Rio de Janeiro. Despite criticisms about its having produced watered-down resolutions and very little concrete action, the summit was nevertheless a historic event, which brought worldwide attention to environmental issues. It was encouraging to see scientists, politicians, humanitarians, and visionaries from throughout the world join forces to help the environment. Members at the summit reported feeling that, despite individual differences of culture and language, there was an underlying understanding that we are all together on one planet facing the same crisis. Groundwork was laid, and a template was created during the summit for shifts in environmental policy throughout the world.

CREATING THE FUTURE

Psychics and scientists have a difficult time predicting the future, but it is known that we are approaching one of the most challenging centuries of human history, which will require a global vision and a unified striving toward common solutions. Instead of predicting the future, we should focus on inventing it. We may not know the answers to the great challenges we face, but it is essential that we release pessimism and replace it with intelligence, faith, and vision, and do everything we can to empower the future. The bottom line is, if there is going to be a cataclysm, we have no control over when or where it will be safe. What we do have control over is what we do and what we think and how it affects the people around us now and the generations to come.

We need to say collectively, "Yes, we care about the earth, and we want it to survive." This requires global vision in a way that we have never had before. Instead of worrying about dire predictions, we need to think about two hundred years in the future or even two thousand years in the future. We can learn from the Iroquois confederation and their requirement that all tribal councils consider the impact of their decisions on the seven generations to follow.

As imperfect as humans are, we are still a precious and unique form of life in the universe. Perhaps it is a bit egocentric to hope for the survival of human beings into the second and third millennium and beyond, considering that ninety-nine percent of all the life that has ever existed on our planet is now extinct. But I would like to think that what we do here and now sends an energy forward that will have an impact thousands of years into the future. It is not inconceivable that this could happen. Collectively, we can make a difference.

Helping the Ecology of the Planet

To make a positive contribution to the ecology of the future, the first step is to educate yourself, your friends, and your family about the environment. Find out about global warming, the ozone layer, deforestation, overpopulation, and species extinction. Projecting for a positive future doesn't mean putting your head under a pillow and denying the reality of the world. It would be naive not to think that we are encountering great difficulties on our planet. There is overwhelming evidence of worldwide industrial pollution affecting our land, air, and sea. The "greenhouse effect" is real. The sea is so polluted that even deep-water fish are showing signs of contamination. Seals and dolphins, all at the top of the food chain, show mutation from pollutants. Chemicals used by farmers are leaching into our rivers, reservoirs, and even our drinking water. Air quality has been affected worldwide to such an extent that even in vast wilderness areas frogs are dying because their thin skins make them susceptible to airborne pollutants. Acid rain and deforestation have become facts of life. It is valuable to find out where we are now environmentally as a planet. Educating yourself and others can help you to come up with and contribute real answers for the future. Arm yourself with knowledge instead of fear.

An alternative to fearing for the environment is seeing the potential for magic, goodness, and great positive change in the times that lie ahead; seeing them not as the end of the world but as the end of the world as we now know it, so that we can create a better, fairer, more beautiful world. When you resist the rampant fear and resulting apathy that is everywhere around you, you are performing an act of power.

When just one person chooses to stand strong, to choose hope over despair, a small but very powerful change is made in the current of the collective unconscious. This choice acts like a magnet, and others, who were perhaps undecided or wavering in their wish to stand strong, are encouraged and strengthened in their resolve. These kinds of courageous acts can result in a magnificent ripple effect, extending far beyond the wildest imagination of the first person who chose to stand up and be accountable. When you decide to believe in a bright future instead of listening to predictions of gloom and doom, you are co-creating the reality of that future for all of us.

Making a Stand

In every moment of your life, be ready to contradict the prevailing notions that the world is coming to an end. Because this belief is so widespread, doomsday comments have infiltrated our language and thinking. When you hear people talking as though life will not be going on much longer, speak up. Be considerate, but let them know that you really don't feel that way. Others are waiting for you to do this. They, too, want to choose hope, but they are afraid of sounding silly, being called a Pollyanna. When you speak out, they lose their fear. They feel validated in their secret, hopeful hearts, so that soon they will be speaking up, too.

Forty years ago in the United States, it was very common

to hear disparaging ethnic and sexual comments that put down various people because of their race, country of origin, or gender. No one thought much about that kind of thing, even though many of these comments were extremely hurtful to their targets. But because no one spoke up to complain, people thought they just had to accept that this was a normal part of conversation, even though privately they might have felt very offended.

But then a few people did start speaking up. At first, they seemed extreme, but the practice gained momentum, and now it is very awkward when someone makes a joke or comment that targets a particular racial or other group of people; to do so has become socially unacceptable. Some may argue that the pendulum of political correctness in the United States has now swung too far the other way, but they might look back on how recently it was that the meanest remarks of this kind could be said in public with impunity.

A few people speaking from their hearts inspire others, who, in turn, pass the message on to those they know. The progression is phenomenal. One person does make a difference! Many of the great movements of history didn't always start out the way they are reported in the history books, where only the actions of kings and warriors and the dates of great battles are recorded. Often the impetus that started those battles and moved those kings to action started in small villages all over the land, where neighbors talked together about their problems and what they thought ought to happen about them.

Change often starts at the grassroots level and moves upward. That's what makes great movements great—they have the support of huge numbers of people. What can start out as a gentle ripple gains momentum until it is a great tidal wave able to move mountains! You can be the little ripple that starts it all. What you think, what you hope for, the tiny actions that you take today, do make a difference. Never discount your ability to effect huge and lasting change. You may never know the full extent of your actions, but you can always know that you did your best, that you listened to your heart and had the faith and courage to carry out what it told you to do. As the Ethiopian proverb says: "When spiderwebs unite, they can tie up a lion."

Working for Causes You Believe In

Many rights and advantages of modern life that we take for granted are in actuality a part of the spiritual legacy handed down to us through the efforts of our own ancestors who worked for causes *they* believed in. The fact that women have the right to vote, the advances made in the fields of civil rights and child labor, and the eight-hour workday—these rights are the direct result of our ancestors working to make the world a better place for us. A sense of gratitude for what we have received can increase our faith in what we, too, can accomplish. It can help increase our own ability to pass on a better world to those who will follow us. Working for a cause about which you are passionate leaves a legacy for those who follow you just as our ancestors left spiritual legacies for us.

SMALL STEPS MAKE A DIFFERENCE

One of the biggest blocks to working for causes you believe in is the feeling that no action you can personally take will be big enough to make a difference. In our busy lives, most of us do not have the time or energy to devote ourselves full-time to any one cause, let alone take on everything that we know is wrong in the world. There may be many issues that we care about, but we have bills to pay, families to feed, demanding jobs that take up most of our time. In the face of these real demands on our time and resources, we sometimes feel guilty that we are not doing more. This can make us feel powerless, which can sometimes lead us into doing nothing at all.

One of the best ways of dealing with these feelings is by taking small, positive steps. Do what you can with what you have and where you are in your life. If you can send only a small amount of money to a cause you care about, if you can donate only an hour a month to making fund-drive calls for an organization you believe in, if you pick up a piece of litter on the side of the road, you have still made a real difference in the balance of the future. You are not alone. You don't need to take large steps since small actions add up to big results. There is a link between the ethical choices we make on a daily basis, which may seem small and inconsequential, and the apparently large choices made by forces beyond our control. Every small choice makes a difference, and *failing* to make the small choices makes a difference as well.

Follow your heart. Find causes that inspire your passion. Involve yourself to the extent that you can, and banish guilt! Feeling guilty that you aren't doing more will only discourage you and tend to make you do less. Praise yourself generously for whatever you are able to contribute. You are making a difference. Whatever contribution you are able to make is vital to the results you are trying to achieve. Who knows the extent of the influence that your actions will have? Everyone remembers Gandhi's role in freeing India from British rule, but without the thousands and thousands of individuals who supported him with their small, individual acts, freedom for India would never have become a reality.

NO ONE PERSON CAN DO IT ALL

No one can do it all. Just pick the parts that make you feel good, and celebrate what you are able to accomplish in those areas. I run my business and do my writing from my home. It is amazing how much paper these two activities generate every week. Since I live in a city that picks up recyclable materials from right outside my door, it takes very little effort on my part to set out that paper. But every week I imagine the new paper products and other useful things that will be made out of the paper I am sending off to be recycled. I see the tall, lovely trees whose lives have been spared by this one small action, and it makes me feel great! Obviously, I'm no hero just because I throw my paper into the recycling bin instead of the rubbish bin that sits right next to it, but I feel like one. My weekly contribution to reducing waste and saving trees isn't going to keep the old-growth forests intact all by itself, but it is part of a movement growing in that direction.

When you take the bus to work instead of driving, you are making a difference. You also can relax and read a favorite book instead of feeling stressed in traffic jams. When you buy organic vegetables at your local supermarket, you are helping to clean up the earth and are also helping to support a small, worker-run business. But at the same time, you are making your own body stronger and more vibrant. Each of the choices that we make in a positive direction sends energy out into the future to bless our descendants, even as it enriches and blesses our lives now.

And every small act that we take in this way is helping to set major social forces in action. Your choice to buy organic food creates a demand that enables and encourages more farmers to produce this chemical-free product. When you buy recycled products, you probably don't usually imagine the effect this is having on people making choices in places far away from you, but it does. Take time consciously to imagine the positive effects your actions are having toward creating a world you can be proud to pass on to your children. Every time you perform a small act in this way, every time you stop and visualize the results of good work, you are creating powerful ripples in the collective unconscious, ripples of joy and hope and inspiration. This is one of the most effective ways of breaking out of negative cycles of frustration and despair.

RELEASE GUILT

It is very important to avoid the pitfall of feeling guilty that you can't do more. If the time you spend driving to work alone in your car is essential to your peace of mind, if that is a time when you are able to center yourself in a way that would be impossible if you were sharing space with others on a crowded city bus, don't feel guilty! It is not possible for any of us to do it all. When we start feeling that we should, then often we feel so discouraged that we may even decrease our efforts. The particular ways of helping that call out to us are the ones that are right for us. The areas that increase our joy in living and energy are the ones where we will be most effective. If you are resenting your contribution, you will definitely not be helping to create positive energy in that area. Your resentment may even lessen the effectiveness of those around you.

Also, if you become too rigid about following new routines, this can backfire as well. Be gentle with yourself. Start out with small commitments that you are sure you can keep. That way you will be able to receive the maximum benefits of increased self-worth and happiness. If you make an overwhelming commitment, such as "I will never buy any non-organic or non-recyclable products," and you are not able to follow through on this intention, then you will feel guilty and inadequate. Try instead to say, "I'm not sure I always want to buy recycled toilet paper, but I will buy organic fresh vegetables when I shop at the supermarket twice a month." That way when you have to rush out to the local corner shop for non-organic broccoli for a last-minute dinner, you won't have to feel that you are breaking your commitment. You will instead feel good every time you follow through on what you know you can do.

And when you do fail, as we all do from time to time, be gentle with yourself. Know that imperfection is what makes humans interesting, so let it go and start again. Your intention and your overall direction are what matter, not each little step one way or the other along the path.

CHOOSE A PLAN OF ACTION

Just as the problems confronting us are enormous, so, too, are the number of ways we can work for solutions. There are as many ways to help out and make a difference as there are individuals. If you look at the whole problem all at once and at everything that needs to be done, you will probably feel overwhelmed and that there's no point in beginning. But there is a much better approach that is exciting and empowering. Ask yourself what you love doing. What changes could you participate in that would be fun and that would fulfill secret urges you may have had for years? Do you love working with people and enjoy organizing things? Then how about volunteering to help run a local benefit to raise money for a cause you believe in? Are you an under-appreciated artist? Call up an organization that does work that excites your imagination and offer to create a poster for their next fund-raising drive. Or donate one of your sculptures to their next auction.

Take time to sit down and come up with a realistic, joy-filled, and empowering action plan. Look at your life to see where you would like to make changes—this week, this month, in the next decade. What would make you feel better and, at the same time, create a better reality for all of us? This can be a very fun project. We all have dreams and aspirations, the callings of our higher self. Often these nudgings from spirit coincide with things we believe could make the world a better place. Each of us is indispensable in creating a bright future. We all have gifts unique only to us that are fundamentally necessary pieces in the building of this new reality. The ways that we feel called upon to help are the best ones for us. What we can do is enough; it is what we should be doing. If you are a single mother raising four children, don't feel guilty that you don't have time to volunteer at the homeless shelter. Your part in creating a beautiful world is in keeping four more young people safe and out of shelters! That is enough; that is fantastic!

KEEP YOUR FOCUS ON THE GOAL

A pitfall in working for causes you believe in is the tendency to focus on what is wrong. If you are working to save the rain-forests, for example, it is easy to focus on how terrible the current level of devastation is. Statistics about how many acres of forest are being destroyed every day are readily available. These statistics are real and they are sobering, but they can also make one feel overwhelmed. Whatever cause you are working for, instead of thinking about how horrible the situation presently is, you can instead visualize the results that you want to achieve. If you are working to save the rainforests, for example, take some time whenever you send in a donation to your organization (or contribute in whatever way you have chosen to support this cause) to visualize endless stretches of beautiful, dense, green, and healthy forests filled with flowers and animals and vibrant life. Know that your actions, however small, are bringing the reality of this vision one step closer to reality. This kind of visualization will make your efforts much more powerful. You will then be able to feel your life as enhanced and more full, instead of depleted and powerless. And the energy that you expend will be part of the legacy that you are leaving to your descendants.

Remember to keep your sights set on the goals you are trying to reach, rather than on the discouraging statistics and grim realities that may have prompted you to act. It is a fact in sports, art, and the martial arts, as well as many other disciplines, that focusing on what you want to achieve and really visualizing that result actually enhances your ability to accomplish your goal. Looking at where you are instead of where you are going only gets you bogged down and entangled in the difficulties of the journey. Keep your eyes on the results you desire!

ADOPT AN ATTITUDE OF JOY

We tend to think that contributing to the future is serious business. We do have serious issues to address on our planet, but being overly worried and concerned can contribute to the problems ahead. Seriousness can sometimes damage your effectiveness, while joy can open you to new energies so that you become much more effective in all the actions that you take. Serious people can't laugh or dance or play. They become imprisoned in their beliefs and decisions. They lose their ability to make a powerful impact.

I've met many very serious people, from environmentalists to New Age adherents, who are "working to save the planet." Though they are obviously sincere in their efforts, I find that I have to remind myself constantly of the value of their message because my spirit shrinks away from the serious self-importance of these individuals. Often I come away feeling exhausted rather than exhilarated and inspired.

However, when I meet someone who is enthusiastic and happy, I want to support that individual to the ends of the earth. We are drawn to individuals who exude joy and who know how to laugh at themselves and life. Laughter brings energy and vitality to everyone around you. To make a difference in the world, be happy. Spread love and laughter and joy wherever you go. Plant flowers. Fly kites. Be kind to strangers. Dance in the rain. Be creative. Appreciate all that is beautiful and good about our planet. This kind of joy is infectious. It will spread from you in ever-increasing circles. What if all the world's leaders were joyous? Would someone who was truly happy start a war? Would someone who was happy hurt another human being?

We are in a crisis, the most serious crisis our planet has faced. This cannot be denied. However, it takes courageous individuals to see the problems and yet disconnect themselves from worry and self-importance in order to live joyously. This can be done. You may need to exorcise your inner demons and heal old family wounds to find your joy, but it is incredibly important that you do this. By reaching into your soul and remembering who you are, you create one of the most powerful forces in the universe. In your inner depths, you are spirit, infinite and holy. The more compassion, understanding, and joy you feel, the more you can make a difference in the future of the world.

CONTRIBUTING TO THE COLLECTIVE UNCONSCIOUS

When you adopt an attitude of joy and learn how to express yourself spontaneously so that your life-force energies aren't repressed, you contribute this energy to the collective unconscious. This in turn contributes to the planet. The great Swiss psychoanalyst Carl Jung wrote extensively about the existence of the phenomenon he called the collective unconscious. Throughout his work over many years, Jung observed the same symbols recurring in people's dreams and imaginations time and time again. After much research, Jung concluded that these symbols are universal and that they have been shared by human beings throughout time. For example, the same themes show up all over the world in the traditional stories of peoples from cultures otherwise unrelated to each other. Also, the same visual symbols have been used to represent similar phenomena by people throughout time. Jung referred to these universal symbols and themes as archetypes.

Jung believed that the collective unconscious is a kind of composite of all human experience, and that each of us shares in this experience. He felt that individual consciousness springs from a primordial human consciousness. Although we all have individual memories and experiences that are recorded in our personal unconscious, the collective unconscious relates to the primordial memories shared by all of us. The collective unconscious is not a static phenomenon. We are all constantly co-creating its content through the influence of our personal thoughts, fears, hopes, dreams, and actions. In a subtle yet profound way, we are all continually both being influenced by the contents of the collective unconscious and are, in turn, influencing it.

You can positively impact the collective unconscious through your positive thoughts and creative actions. The love, understanding, and joy you feel creates an energy that positively influences others, because we are not separate from each other, from our friends, our communities, our cultures, and our planet. We all are interrelated, and we each can make a difference through our attitude toward life. A powerful way to impact the collective unconscious is by holding a vision for the future.

WHAT IS YOUR EXPECTATION FOR THE FUTURE OF CIVILIZATION?

In order to project your energy into a vision for the future, it is first valuable to assess what your current attitudes and underlying beliefs concerning the future of the world are. There is no way to know for sure what the future will hold. We can't control the future; however, we can control what we believe in right now. And the beliefs and expectations we currently hold can help shape the future. The expectations and beliefs that motivate you aren't necessarily the ones that you consciously believe; they are the ones that reside in your subconscious mind. The exercise below is designed to help you discover your underlying expectations. In preparation for the exercise, ask yourself, "What is my expectation for the years ahead? Do I see human beings surviving on the planet in five years? Ten years? Fifty years? One hundred years? Five hundred years? One thousand years?" (The planet will survive, the question is, Do you believe humans will survive?) If you discover that you believe in a worldwide cataclysm or a short-lived future for the planet, notice the reasons that you have for this opinion. When observing your opinion about the future of the earth, try to balance the drama of a belief in an apocalypse against the value of believing in a positive, vibrant future. On page 197 is an exercise to help you evaluate what your underlying beliefs are.

From any given point in time, there are many possible changes radiating out like the spokes of a wagon wheel. When you imagine traveling into the future in your time machine, you are journeying down one future probability. If you saw a future that you were not happy with, repeat the exercise again and journey to another probable future, until you have tracked one that is positive. Then hold a strong vision of it; this can help bring it about.

Exercise: Discovering Your
Expectations for the Future

Imagine that there is a small time machine in your home. Enter the time machine, and set the dial for one year in the future. Step out of the time machine, and walk through your home, stopping to look out of the windows. Finally, open the front door and notice what you see. Does it look about the same as it does now, or have things changed over the year? If there is vegetation that can be seen from your front door, has it grown any taller? Get back in your time machine, and set the dial for five years into the future. Once again, get out of your machine and look through the windows and open the door of your home and notice what you see. Step back into the time machine, and push the dial ahead twenty years. Don't be concerned if the building changes, you are safe inside your time machine.

Each time you step out of the machine, time stands still so you can observe the future in ease and comfort. Continue to move forward in time,

---

observing how your environment changes. When
you have finished your observations of the future,
set the dial to your present time and bring yourself
back to the present.

A VISION FOR THE FUTURE

You have a remarkable ability to access the inner resources
within you, the outer forces around you, and your connection
to the cosmos for the benefit of the planet. Activating the creative power of the mind by simply relaxing, visualizing, and
focusing can generate a powerful and positive energy that will
emanate from you.

A number of years ago, a remarkable experiment took
place in Brighton, a city on the south coast of England. A
number of individuals, who were very concerned about the
world, sat down and discussed what they could do that would
help make a difference. These people believed in the power of
meditation and visualization, so they decided that for a few
minutes every day they would all send thoughts of peace to a
central place in Brighton. The central point they chose was a
fountain, to which they consistently sent energy for one year.
At the end of the year, they wondered, "Have we made a
difference? Have our efforts helped the community?" They
decided that the way they could determine this was to compare statistics from the years before their experiment with the

twelve months they spent sending loving energy to the fountain. What they found was remarkable. Emergency admissions into the hospitals were reduced. Crime was down. Car accidents had decreased. The results were so encouraging that news of their experiment spread. Not long afterward, Fountain Groups (as they became called) mushroomed all over England and eventually spread to other parts of the world. Wherever they were formed, the results reported were the same. Through focusing on peace, a difference was made.

I believe in the power of meditation and prayer. I believe our positive thoughts can make a difference to our communities and to our planet. A cynic, on the other hand, might believe that meditation and visualization couldn't possibly bring crime down or couldn't possibly affect a town or community. However, even if I am wrong (and I don't believe that I am), and even if spending a couple of minutes a day thinking positive and peaceful thoughts doesn't have far-reaching effects, there is still value in meditation. One person who feels more inner peace and is more relaxed has a positive effect on each of the people with whom he or she comes in contact, and this, in turn, makes a contribution to the planet. In other words, you don't have anything to lose by sending loving thoughts out into the world, and perhaps there is much to be gained.

Although it may be difficult to project your imagination far into the future, there is great value in attempting to do so. Imagining and holding a vision of a positive future can help make it a reality. The next exercise is important. It can make an enormous difference to our planetary future. As you project your energy and love into the future, you can create a ripple that can be felt on the farthest shores of humanity.

In addition to holding a vision for the future and sending

peace to those who follow you, you may want to consider gathering with like-minded individuals once a month to visualize for peace together. Or you may want to act like the Fountain Groups and once a day send thoughts of peace to a focal point in your hometown.

---

*Exercise: Projecting Energy
into the Future*

In this exercise you will imagine or create a vision for the future: your personal vision, a worldwide vision, and a vision for your descendants. Imagine yourself in the future. Draw a floor plan of the home you would like to live in in ten years, twenty years, thirty years. Imagine yourself walking around each of the rooms. Visualize the area outdoors as well. Visualize the life that you are leading that places you in such a home. Notice how you feel in this home. Once you feel excited and energized by what you see, plant or anchor the feeling associated with this home in your body. To do this, first locate the positive feeling, then notice where in your body it resides. (Every emotion has an associated body location.) Then expand the feeling. Let it grow inside you until it seems to fill you. By doing this, you are anchoring the feeling in your body. It is much easier to meet and create

---

your future when you have the feeling associated with the future event planted in your subconscious. Once a desire has been firmly planted, it demands some sort of response from the universe.

After you have created a personal vision, visualize the world in ten years, twenty years, thirty years, and beyond. Use the same process as above for anchoring the feeling. Hold a vision for the future as bright, shining, and exhilarating for all inhabitants of the planet.

Now travel down the cord of time to your descendants, both your immediate descendants and your faraway descendants seven generations down to road. See them living in joy and harmony on a planet that supports all life in a humane and gracious manner.

There is enormous power in your visions and in your willingness to visualize and project energy into the future. You can make a difference!

GATEWAY TO THE FUTURE

The urgency of the spiritual and environmental crises that face humanity requires bold and visionary methods. Through radically expanding your horizons to include your descendants and your ancestors, by creating new myths for the millennium and developing a legacy for your progeny, there is hope for the future. The greatest purveyor of hope for the twenty-first century is faith. I have faith in a loving and compassionate Creator, and I believe that our lives and our destinies are guided. Our children and grandchildren will face challenges in the future; however, I believe that with faith and passion we can create a legacy that will shine through the years ahead and beyond.

We *can* make a wonderful world to pass on to our descendants. Maybe not all at once with a snap of our fingers, but we really can do it. We will need to have faith; we will have to summon up our courage; we will have to be creative. We will also have to listen to our hearts and follow their yearnings. But this will not only create the reality that we want to pass on but will also enrich our own lives immeasurably in the present. Our efforts need not be perfect to be sufficient. All our actions together, all our hopes and dreams surging into a mighty river of consciousness, can create a better world, one we can look forward to, where our children's children can live and love, right on down to the seventh generation and beyond. I can see this future cresting on the horizon, and I am filled with joy at its prospect.

Notes

Chapter 1

1. C. Jung, *Modern Man in Search of His Soul* (New York: Harcourt, Brace, 1936), 125–6.

Chapter 3

1. David Gelman and Debra Rosenberg, "Family Secrets," *Newsweek* 129, no. 8 (Febuary 24, 1997): 26–30.

2. Ibid.

3. Ibid.

Chapter 5

1. Joseph Campbell, *Hero with a Thousand Faces*, 2d ed. (Princeton: Princeton University Press, 1968), 3.

2. Ibid., 11.

3. *Reader's Digest*, February 1988.

4. Joseph Campbell, *Primitive Mythology* (New York: Penguin Books, 1976), 60–61.

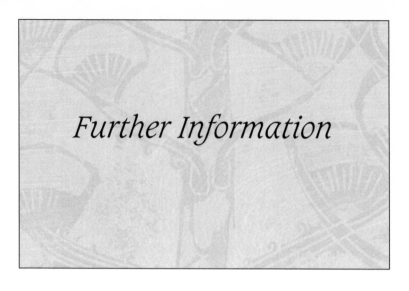

Further Information

Denise offers professional certification training programs in Interior Alignment© as well as seminars and workshops on other subjects.

For information about Denise's seminars in the United States or for Denise's audio and video tapes contact:
Denise Linn Seminars
P.O. Box 75657
Seattle, Washington 98125-0657, USA

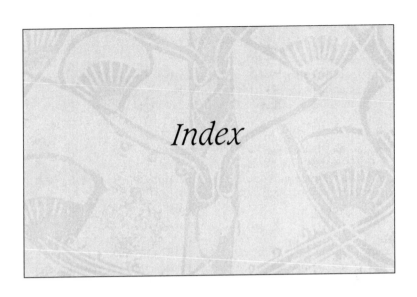

Index